South Africa's Struggle
for Human Rights

OHIO SHORT HISTORIES OF AFRICA

This series of Ohio Short Histories of Africa is meant for those who are looking for a brief but lively introduction to a wide range of topics in South African history, politics, and biography, written by some of the leading experts in their fields.

Steve Biko
by Lindy Wilson
ISBN: 978-0-8214-2025-6
e-ISBN: 978-0-8214-4441-2

Spear of the Nation (Umkhonto weSizwe):
South Africa's Liberation Army, 1960s–1990s
by Janet Cherry
ISBN: 978-0-8214-2026-3
e-ISBN: 978-0-8214-4443-6

Epidemics:
The Story of South Africa's Five Most Lethal Human Diseases
by Howard Phillips
ISBN: 978-0-8214-2026-3
e-ISBN: 978-0-8214-4443-6

South Africa's Struggle for Human Rights
by Saul Dubow
ISBN: 978-0-8214-2027-0
e-ISBN: 978-0-8214-4440-5

South Africa's Struggle for Human Rights

Saul Dubow

OHIO UNIVERSITY PRESS

ATHENS

Ohio University Press, Athens, Ohio 45701
www.ohioswallow.com

First published as *A Brief History of Rights in South Africa*
by Jacana Media (Pty) Ltd in 2012
10 Orange Street
Sunnyside
Auckland Park 2092
South Africa
(+27 11) 628-3200
www.jacana.co.za

To obtain permission to quote, reprint, or otherwise reproduce or
distribute material from Ohio University Press publications, please
contact our rights and permissions department at (740) 593-1154 or
(740) 593-4536 (fax).

First published in North America in 2012 by Ohio University Press
Printed in the United States of America
Ohio University Press books are printed on acid-free paper ⊗ ™

20 19 18 17 16 15 14 13 12   5 4 3 2 1

ISBN: 978-0-8214-2027-0
e-ISBN: 978-0-8214-4440-5

Library of Congress Cataloging-in-Publication Data
Dubow, Saul.
 South Africa's struggle for human rights / Saul Dubow.
     p. cm. — (Ohio short histories of Africa)
 Includes bibliographical references and index.
 ISBN 978-0-8214-2027-0 (pb : alk. paper) —
     ISBN 978-0-8214-4440-5
1. Human rights—South Africa—History. 2. Civil rights—South
Africa—History. 3. Democracy—South Africa. 4. South Africa—
Politics and government. I. Title.
JC599.S5D83 2012
 323.0968—dc23
                              2012027269

Cover design by Joey Hi-Fi

Contents

Preface

The immediate spur to writing this book was an invitation by my friend and colleague Paul Betts to write an article on human rights and social rights for a conference he was helping to organise in Berlin in 2010. Snow-bound Britain prevented our reaching Germany, and I was left with an incomplete paper requiring a great deal more work. In doing this, I began to realise that the issues explored here also have deeper roots: this book is in some ways a companion piece to my contribution on 'South Africa and South Africans' in the new *Cambridge History of South Africa*, volume 2 (2011); it may also have been sparked by a late-night argument with a spirited political activist and close friend (circa 1980) about the extent to which the ANC's 'Charterist' tradition entailed a commitment to rights.

Whatever its origins, this short volume would not have emerged in the form that it has without the imagination and encouragement of my publisher Russell Martin. Although this is only a small book, I have incurred an unusually long list of debts in producing it. Colin Bundy, Trevor Burnard, Wayne Dooling, Gail Gerhart, Hermann Giliomee, Patrick Harries, Mark Mazower, Sam Moyn, Keith Shear, Milton Shain, Rob Skinner, André du Toit, and Clive Webb all made very helpful – and sometimes challenging – suggestions. Since the subject intrudes into specialist areas of law that are not the usual domain of historians, I also sought the advice of Richard Wilson and Hugh Corder, both of whom generously gave me time and set me right without making me feel an interloper. I am deeply grateful for all this help and friendship. While the doctrine of collective responsibility might conceivably apply, it would not be fair to implicate them in the outcome.

1

Introduction

South Africa's transition to a post-apartheid democracy, so often referred to as a 'miracle', is widely celebrated as a triumph for global human rights. The country's new Constitution, its Truth and Reconciliation Commission, and the moral authority of Nelson Mandela stand as exemplary proof of this achievement. Yet, less than a generation after the achievement of freedom, the status of human rights in South Africa is uncertain. In government, the ANC has displayed an inconsistent attitude to the protection, let alone advancement, of hard-won freedoms and rights, and it is not at all clear that a broader civic and political consciousness of the importance of rights is rooting itself more widely in popular culture.

South Africa's final Constitution was intended to aid in the establishment of a post-apartheid society based on democratic values, social justice and fundamental human rights. In doing so, it was designed not only to defend 'natural rights' and restrict the powers of the state over the individual, but also to play a role in building an open, democratic society, holding the government to account where necessary. The Constitutional Court's senior judges have stressed the need for the Constitution to be 'interpreted generously to achieve its purposes', which include social transformation.[1]

Realisation of these ideals depends on the state's active engagement in expanding the domain of rights for the collective social well-being of the people. Yet, a government which came to power proclaiming its commitment to 'second-generation' social rights frequently finds itself blocking their active realisation. In power, leading government figures have shown increasing lack of regard for the independence of the judiciary, and high-level corruption suggests that the well-being of the elite prevails over the wider interests of the people. In the view of Arthur Chaskalson, first President of the country's Constitutional Court and Chief Justice until 2005, corruption and the 'fragility of rights' are two linked dangers which have to be confronted. A similar point is made by the writer and public intellectual Njabulo Ndebele, speaking in 2011: 'The greatest threat we face is the impact on the public mind of the emergent, unconstitutional culture of concealment.'[2]

10

South Africa offers a unique case study for historians of human rights. Its extended colonial history invites us to consider the development of several competing rights 'regimes' – liberal, Afrikaner, and African nationalist – whose political salience can be broadly correlated with distinct phases of political power.[3] It is indeed hard to think of any other colonised society where distinct strands of rights discourse have been conjoined in this manner. Most histories of human rights are located at the international level. To be able to locate these different rights traditions in the national narratives of a single society presents particular challenges.

Although the struggles against British imperialism, Afrikaner nationalism and white supremacy were configured broadly to achieve 'rights' (or to redress 'wrongs'), the phrase 'human rights' seldom features in either the texts or the indexes of key works of history. This immediately raises the question about the status of rights in South African history. The premise here is that struggles over rights in South Africa have helped to shape its emergence as a nation-state over a long period, though there is no suggestion that the objective of securing rights has been consistent or that rights claims have always been to the fore. In exploring how deeply entrenched rights thinking is in South African political thought, this book makes two claims which, on the surface, may seem contradictory: first, that a legacy of rights thinking – however episodic, fragmented or attenuated – *can* usefully be traced back over two centuries in South Africa; and second, that the embrace of human rights discourse by South Africans in the post-1990 era is, notwithstanding the former claim, surprising.

The term 'human rights' is difficult to track with precision, in part because the formulation is anachronistic and has come to acquire a much more expanded meaning in recent years, but also because its usage is unstable and not conducive to rigorous definition. The domain of rights overlaps with concepts of citizenship, constitutionalism, natural rights, civil rights, minority rights and the 'rule of law'.[4] It is coextensive with a long tradition of theological thought around human dignity and the integrity of the person. And it is also interwoven with claims to social rights, which are nowadays seen as a natural extension of first-generation rights – unlike the situation in South Africa under segregation and apartheid, when they were offered as *substitutes* for civic and political freedoms.

That the apartheid government exhibited active hostility to the concept of individual human rights is undeniable. This attitude followed from the brand of conservative anti-humanism and neo-Calvinism which led its ideologues to equate the notion of liberal rights-bearing individuals as a fearsome challenge to God's primacy and therefore as coextensive with other secular heresies, communism most especially.

The first apartheid government came to power in 1948, the same year that the United Nations adopted its Universal Declaration of Human Rights. Already the target of severe criticism by the General Assembly, South Africa was one of only a very few countries that refused to ratify the UN Declaration, a decision that helped to single it out as an international pariah. South Africa was not the only country in the world to deny rights to its citizens but it was alone in according rights to only some of its citizens. Within the country, the new apartheid government used the law to roll out its radical programme of racial exclusion. When the law stood in its way, as was the case in 1955–6 when the removal of Coloureds from the common voters' roll conflicted with entrenched clauses of the 1909 South Africa Act, constitutional protections were simply swept away. Throughout its period in power the apartheid government displayed unremitting hostility towards civil liberties.

The African National Congress (ANC), by contrast, claimed political rights from its foundation in 1912 and espoused wider democratic rights from the 1940s, in line with its reading of the Atlantic Charter of 1941.

But its commitment to this ideal receded from the mid-1950s, just as Coloureds were losing all vestiges of their voting rights, and it was only in the mid-1980s that the organisation's active engagement with rights revived. This renders questionable the repeated claim by the ANC politician and legal specialist Kader Asmal that South Africa's post-apartheid Constitution is a logical outcome of the ANC's long 'human rights tradition'.[5] The teleological implications of this telescoped history are difficult to sustain. It would be historically more accurate to say that the 1980s saw the ANC reclaiming an inheritance that it had distanced itself from for at least 30 years. This legacy was substantially shaped by an eclectic mix of liberal, humanist, Gandhian and social democratic ideas with which it had grown acutely uncomfortable, especially during its long period of existence underground and in exile from 1960.

Thus, if there was one issue uniting Afrikaner and African nationalisms through most of the second half of the 20th century, and throughout the Cold War, it was a mutual suspicion of liberal ideology and of individual-based human rights. A decade before the 1994 accord which formally ended apartheid, it would have been impossible to imagine – let alone to predict – that the accord would be substantially based on a shared acceptance of political (and economic) liberal tenets grounded in a new global vogue for rights and constitutionalism.[6] This required two antagonistic nationalist movements, proceeding from different premises and with differing objectives in mind, to rethink their respective pasts in order to conceive of a common future.

Perhaps this late embrace of human rights is not so surprising. In a major new study Samuel Moyn argues that the emergence of modern human rights thinking as a global phenomenon can be dated only from the 1970s. They came 'seemingly from nowhere'. Moyn also notes, in passing, that not enough is known about the 'changing terms of resistance to apartheid in South Africa' as regards the shift from an 'anticolonialist optic' to a 'human rights struggle'.[7] By contrast, Robin Blackburn's rebuttal of Moyn's 'magic moment' approach reinstates a much longer history going back to the Enlightenment, highlighting anti-colonial and anti-slavery movements in particular. For Blackburn, the 'struggle against apartheid South Africa was an icon of the anti-imperialist movement and surely had an absolute claim to the banner of human rights.'[8] Elizabeth Borgwardt, similarly, identifies Nelson Mandela as a key interpreter of the modern view of human rights when she counterposes the 1941 Atlantic Charter of Mandela's 'aspirations' (namely, a global statement of universal principles applying to individuals as well as nations) to the much more restrictive Charter of Winston Churchill's 'intentions'.[9]

This book seeks to fill in the gap identified by Moyn in respect of the history of political thought in South Africa. It is in broad agreement with Moyn that the mid-1970s was a key moment in the process of linking anti-apartheid struggles to the international human rights movement, which, as Karel Vasek argued in 1977, was then entering its third-generational phase as 'rights of solidarity'.[10] It also seeks, like Blackburn, to redress the European- and American-centric ways in which the intellectual history of human rights is so often written, albeit by avoiding the inference that the liberation movement in South Africa was wholly committed to the banner of human rights. This entails reading traditions of human rights thought over more than two centuries with an emphasis on the ways in which ideas, circulating in a global sphere and with claims to universality, were adopted and reshaped for particular uses in local contexts.

2

Burgher republicanism and colonialism

The earliest context in which it makes sense to speak of rights in South Africa relates to citizenship status or 'burgerschap'. At the slave-holding Cape, 'free burghers' were independent colonists, typically 'Boers' (farmers) who succeeded in moving beyond the strict controls of the governing Dutch East India Company (VOC) from the mid-17th century in order to secure effective rights to land.[11] This status (which seems not to have been replicated in other Dutch colonies under VOC control) connoted certain attendant privileges and duties, including payment of taxes, participation in the commando (militia) system, and opportunities to claim land. New research indicates that town-based burghers were able to rise to public office or gain social prestige by acquiring personal wealth, which in some cases proved substantial. In 1778 urban-based burghers at the Cape began a wave of protests against the VOC government during which they claimed the citizenship rights enjoyed by their compatriots elsewhere in the Dutch world.[12]

Yet, however influential, prosperous or respected they may have been, free burghers remained second-class citizens in the sense that they were bound to swear oaths of loyalty and obedience both to the Estates General and to local representatives of the VOC, who invariably outweighed settlers in terms of rank and status.[13] From the beginning of European settlement there was some limited mechanism for burgher representation in the justice system (the Council of Justice) and by the 18th century burgher councillors were able to convene separately from the official Council of Policy while still remaining subordinate to the Company. Their autonomy and effective power probably increased with distance from Cape Town: the expanding network of rural judicial officials (heemraden, veld-cornets and landdrosts) and burgher militias or commandos (led by the commandant) meant that the Cape's burgher gentry remained effectively in control of the countryside until well into the 19th century.[14]

Although free burghers were structurally unequal to the Company and its leading officials, they were not entirely without rights. Roman-Dutch law afforded distinct protections to citizens, including free women, whose status and property rights were probably more secure under Cape jurisprudence than they were in Britain.[15] Burghers were also able to exercise a degree of political influence: for example, colonists' protests against the high-handedness and corruption of Governor Willem Adriaan van der Stel resulted in his discharge from office in 1707. Burghers also cavilled at restrictions on their assumed rights to barter with (or, less decorously, mount raids against) the indigenous Khoekhoen (Hottentots) in search of cattle and pasture. Freedom to treat indigenous peoples with relative impunity formed part of such rights claims. In 1739, a renegade French-speaking soldier, Estienne Barbier, sparked a revolt against Company rule on the part of white frontiersmen who refused to submit to the law when accused of killing Nama along the Orange River and stealing their cattle. Barbier outraged officialdom by pinning his grievances to the door of a church in explicit defiance of a rule forbidding such conduct. For this and other misdemeanours he was subjected to a public judicial execution, his body quartered and displayed along the chief roads of the Colony as a warning to others.[16]

Free-burger hostility to the Company, on the one hand, and to indigenous peoples of the interior, on the other, was a volatile mixture and this was soon ignited by the vapours of republican and Enlightenment ideas drifting across the Atlantic from Europe and North America. Between 1778 and 1787 a group identifying themselves as 'Cape Patriots' provided detailed complaints against Company misrule, asserting a combination of political and economic burgher rights in the name of democratic revolution (their movement was closely informed by anti-Orangist sentiment in the Netherlands).[17] Likewise, in 1795 a group of armed burghers wearing French Revolutionary tricolour cockades took over the rural town of Graaff-Reinet in the name of the people (the *algemene volkstem*). Refusing to submit to the authority of Company rule or to pay taxes, they established a 'national convention'. Much the same occurred closer to Cape Town in the same year when a band of sixty rebels deposed the landdrost at Swellendam.

The objectives of these rebels can hardly be termed emancipatory: in rejecting the jurisdiction of Company rule in Cape Town, they were protesting not only against taxes but also at official restrictions against treating Khoekhoe captive children in effect as slaves. To the extent that the rebels were motivated by republicanism and incipient nationalism, their actions signalled a desire to replace local authority by forging direct links with Holland – a plan that never had much political traction. The historian Hermann Giliomee remarks drily that the brief display of revolutionary cockades was decidedly 'not the dawn of a new democratic scheme of thought on African soil'.[18] Stripped of its ideological colouring and inspiration, their battle was fundamentally rooted in local realities and only to a very limited extent driven by broader idealism.

Such acts of burgher rebellion were in any case gestural and fleeting. The context of anti-Company agitation was forever changed in 1795 when the British temporarily occupied the Cape before transferring it to Batavian rule in 1802. In the interlude before the British took over the Cape once more in 1806, the new Dutch administration sought to achieve significant changes in governance. Inspired by the spirit of the European Enlightenment (the concept of *rechten van den mensch* appeared for the first time in Dutch in 1791),[19] Commissioner-General De Mist's administration worked to transform the economic and political structures of the Cape. An important aspect of the envisaged reforms was the imperative to exert control over the unruly burghers on the Cape frontier and to rein in their persistent maltreatment of indigenous peoples, farm servants as well as tribes-people.

De Mist's enlightened colonial policy was significantly informed by the contemporary writings of the English traveller and official John Barrow, whose influence extended to the British administration at the Cape after 1806.[20] His highly influential two-volume *Travels into the Interior of South Africa* (1801, 1804) – intended both as a scientific audit and as a prospectus for colonisation – traduced Dutch colonists for their indolence, obesity, brutality and moral degradation. Conversely, Barrow defended the 'Hottentots' (Khoekhoen), maintaining they were a mild people who had sunk low in the scale of humanity as a result of suffering from acts of colonial malfeasance at the hands of the Dutch. Barrow was more enamoured of the Xhosa, portraying them as a fine race of men with exquisite physical attributes, who might respond well to the British civilising process.[21] A new constituency of proto-human rights activists were soon to pursue this theory further.

The second British administration at the Cape targeted the mercantilist and slave systems that underpinned Dutch rule as retrogressive evils. Officials in the conservative and militaristic 'second British empire' balked at the idea of extending social and political freedoms, though they were keen to expand economic activity and to regularise systems of administration and justice. In Christopher Bayly's words, 'official despotism' coexisted with a 'supposedly liberal state'.[22] The arrival of new British immigrants from the 1820s especially in the Eastern Cape had the unintended consequence of bringing to the Cape modern social and political ideas minted in centres like Edinburgh and London. Some immigrants immediately began to press for new civic as well as economic freedoms. It is in this context that it becomes possible to talk of citizenship and human rights at the Cape on an expanded scale.

The new anglophone concept of citizenship was by no means coterminous with the burgher concept, which derived from European republican traditions. It primarily denoted rights-bearing citizens who looked to expand their civic freedoms as Cape colonists within the scope of the British colonial state. A secondary, though by no means less important, impulse was associated with natural rights theory or the rights of man. This took form in the context of evangelical campaigns to improve the social, moral and spiritual condition of aboriginal peoples.[23] For analytic purposes these two dimensions of what came to be known as the tradition of Cape liberalism – its non-racial human universalism and its specific claims for civil liberties and colonial citizenship – ought to be kept distinct.

3

Humanitarianism

In the first place, a small but vocal humanitarian and emancipationist lobby became active in advocating the abolition of slavery and measures to free Khoekhoe servants and child 'apprentices' from conditions of effective serfdom. Their networks of influence extended beyond the Cape to mission societies and evangelical campaigning groups in Britain like the Clapham Sect. The centrepiece of this reforming urge was Ordinance 50 (1828) 'for improving the condition of the Hottentots and other free persons of colour at the Cape of Good Hope'. This measure, coinciding with the Charters of Justice (1827 and 1832), which gave rise to an independent judiciary with a Supreme Court, guaranteed equality in law and security of property to all free inhabitants of the Cape irrespective of colour. Ordinance 50 was strongly advocated by proponents of legal equality (and a free labour market) like the Rev. John Philip and his network of associates in the London Missionary Society (LMS), following on from the efforts of the LMS missionaries Johannes van der Kemp and James Read to give servants and captive 'apprentices' protection from their masters. It was given critical support, too, by Andries Stockenström, Commissioner-General for the Eastern Cape, a proto-Afrikaner who took the view that colonists were best protected if rights and privileges were available to all men.[24] Thus, even if the practical benefits of Ordinance 50 are exaggerated – the historian W.M. Macmillan noted in 1927 that it was a form of 'class legislation' which did not place Khoekhoen on a 'footing of absolute equality with the white colonists' – Ordinance 50 nevertheless represented 'a kind of charter of rights' for the Khoekhoen, indeed one whose formulation may have consciously echoed the Magna Carta.[25]

The social gospel practised by leading missionaries like John Philip and Robert Moffat entailed a thorough transformation of their converts' cultural belief system: their determined non-racism coexisted with a cultural determinism that assumed the infinite malleability of human nature under benevolent Christian guidance. Mission stations were turned into model productive communities in places like Theopolis, Bethelsdorp and Kat River, while visible social and economic progress was seen as crucial to proving that converts were 'worthy recipients of the full rights and privileges of citizens'.[26]

Philip's ceaseless campaign to tie the salvation of indigenes' souls to fundamental, if gradual, political and social reform marks an early high-water mark in the effort to secure civil rights, equality of status, and the rule of law. (This explains why the name of Philip, revered by mission-educated indigenes and lionised in liberal evangelical circles, became infamous in generations of settler and Afrikaner historiography.)[27]

It is plausible to see Ordinance 50 as the first clear statement of human rights in South Africa, and to an extent it was, not least in virtue of the way in which it affirmed the humanitarian view, as expressed by Philip, that 'the actual capacity of the African is nothing inferior to that of the European' and therefore that all humans were equal in God's conception.[28] Human rights in this sense amounted to a recognition of universal humanity based in common personhood, whether conceived in religious or racial terms. The connection between human rights and humanitarianism (which has common roots in Enlightenment conceptions of natural law and embodies the assumption that 'all human beings possess rights by virtue of their humanity')[29] is grounded in the desire to promote human welfare and dignity. Yet, as Richard Wilson and Richard Brown demonstrate, the humanitarian impulse to promote welfare and alleviate suffering is not always synonymous with the defence of political

27

or legal rights, since it may be based in a religious ethic of charity or paternalist protection.[30] Notably, missionaries like Philip did make the connection between welfare and rights. Moreover, they achieved the quality of emotional empathy with South Africa's indigenous peoples that, as Lynn Hunt argues, is key to seeing 'others' as part of a common political community.[31]

This recognition, radical as it was, did not necessarily mean social equality or entitlement. For, while Ordinance 50 removed disabilities in order to make persons of colour legally living in the Cape equal *subjects* of the Crown, it did not confer equal rights on citizens in the sense of republican France or America – 'no individual was ever legally a *citizen* of the empire'.[32] The rights discourse surrounding abolitionism at the Cape was, therefore, not revolutionary in the sense that it was in late-18th-century Haiti, which enunciated a vision of rights that long 'haunted' French and British imperial rulers.[33] Reform rather than revolution was always the objective of the humanitarians, whose reference point remained the British imperial state (or Crown), other than when their moral viewpoint transcended such boundaries to include the dominion of God.[34]

The second dimension of the struggle for political rights refers to the activities of new colonists at the

Cape, many of whom arrived in the 1820s as part of immigration schemes geared at settlement in the Eastern Cape along the contested colonial frontier with the Xhosa. This tradition was closely associated with efforts to assert a distinctive or 'particularist' form of expanded 'British' colonial identity, one which was sufficiently capacious to transcend divisions between English and Dutch and which might also extend to deserving non-white citizens too. Thomas Pringle and John Fairbairn, both Scottish immigrants and scions of enlightened Edinburgh, were prominent advocates of such rights. In 1824 they jointly established a newspaper, *The South African Commercial Advertiser*, which frankly asserted their rights as free-born Britons in a new colony of settlement. The publication was promptly shut down by Governor Lord Charles Somerset, a High Tory autocrat, who was instinctively suspicious of any form of radicalism or 'Jacobinism'.

The battle to establish the principle of freedom of the press achieved a notable victory when Pringle and Fairbairn won the right to publish newspapers without executive oversight in 1828. The campaign for freedom of expression was centred on settler colonial civic rights but it also embraced the broader humanitarian struggle to improve the legal and social rights of the indigenous population, in particular the abolition of slavery.[35] In the case of Pringle, who bears the distinction of being South Africa's first poet as well as a powerful proponent of emancipation, the moral purpose of the humanitarians is evoked not only in his political life but also in his literary depictions of 'the enslaved Khoi, the defiant Bushman, and the [Xhosa] revolutionary warrior prophet'.[36]

Tensions between anglophone humanitarian emancipationists and conservative Dutch-speaking slave-holders soon became evident. In particular, the rights of slaves had to be balanced against the property rights of slave-holders, the bulk of whom were Boer farmers. For Fairbairn, whose extensive public career at the Cape drew him into the world of commerce and insurance as well as journalism, abolition and monetary compensation to slave-owners were fully compatible: free labour was more productive than slave labour and financial compensation, which the British government was obliged to offer, would provide new capital for investment. This did not stop Fairbairn falling out with his Dutch counterpart, Christoffel Brand, founder of *De Zuid-Afrikaan*, over abolition and compensation.[37]

Humanitarians also came into conflict with British settlers who struggled through most of the 19th century to extend the frontiers of the Eastern Cape into lands occupied by the Xhosa. In doing so, they sought to impel Africans to enter into service as farm workers.

Whereas English-speaking frontiersmen tended to disparage Dutch-speaking Boers, both groups shared a mutual loathing of the humanitarian lobby. By the 1840s there was strong evidence that the influence of the evangelical humanitarian movement was receding. With this, the religious and humanitarian tradition of rights in the person was refocused on the narrower question of political citizenship.

4

Liberalism and its challenges

The humanitarian impulses of the Cape liberals should not be overestimated: with rare exceptions, liberals were motivated more by the desire to expand the realm of citizenship and rights for white colonists rather than for Africans. The institutions that they so assiduously built – ranging across the fields of commerce, politics, as well as the arts and sciences – were primarily intended to prove that white colonists were respectable middle-class agents of progress. The desire to stimulate trade and economic development formed part of a broad effort to enhance settlers' status as colonial citizens enjoying the rights of free-born Englishmen. These were proto-colonial nationalists whose claims to citizenship rights and representative institutions were strongly inflected by local conditions (above all, the need to incorporate elements of Afrikaner and African society as worthy citizens), such that the accent on the much vaunted phenomenon of

'Cape liberalism' ought to fall as much on its *Capeness* as the extent of its liberality.[38]

Multiple strands of colonial nationalist civic assertion came together in 1849 when local agitation against the Governor's intention to land convicts at the Cape met with a boycott of government institutions, resulting in an unprecedented demonstration of civic national feeling that transcended (white) ethnic and class lines. The *Cape Town Mail* asserted that the struggle had 'created a people in South Africa' for the first time, while Fairbairn's *Commercial Advertiser* argued that by their resistance 'the people of the Cape of Good Hope have shown to the world what it is that constitutes a state'.[39] Dutch-speaking opinion-formers like F.S. Watermeyer and A.N.E. Changuion, representatives of what André du Toit refers to as the Cape Afrikaners' (failed) 'liberal moment', likewise asserted a rhetoric of popular rights at this time.[40] Such claims soon fed into growing demands for political rights (or privileges), consistent with cherished English liberty; these were partly realised in 1853 by the acquisition of Representative Government.

Key to the new constitutional arrangement was a parliament elected on the principle of a non-racial franchise for all qualifying males. The political imperative to ensure that Dutch- and English-speakers qualified for the vote was one major reason why the bar was kept low. Political inclusion of non-white people was, however, only a secondary objective and this principle was heavily conditioned by pragmatism – the so-called safety valve. As the Attorney-General William Porter, an exemplar of the Cape liberal tradition and an architect of the low 1853 franchise, reasoned: 'I would rather meet the Hottentot at the hustings, voting for his representative, than meet the Hottentot in the wilds with his gun upon his shoulder.'[41]

Notably, the 1853 franchise system was one of the most inclusive in the world: its relatively low property qualification (residence in a house valued at £25) was determined by the need to keep the alliance with poorer Dutch-speakers intact. Many Coloureds gained voting rights at this time; they were soon joined by African converts to Christianity like the Mfengu – typically, improving peasants, teachers and preachers – who visibly embraced the tenets of the Christian civilising mission. For such Africans, the citizenship rights associated with the franchise were highly prized: they afforded substantial constitutional protection (for instance, the right to purchase land) and bore incalculable symbolic value as well. But although some voting constituencies were heavily dependent on the African vote, no African or Coloured person ever sat in the Cape Assembly, which remained a white man's preserve.

For a quarter of a century after 1853, Cape liberal ideology endorsed the possibility, even the desirability, of assimilating deserving Africans to European cultural standards. Missionaries, merchants and native administrators were in broad agreement that citizenship rights could be acquired by all men who subscribed to the values of civilisation and progress (measured in moral as well as material terms). This amalgamationist strategy had elements of the carrot and the stick: deserving Africans would be rewarded with the fruits of citizenship and those who refused to abandon their 'tribal' ways or to cooperate with settler colonialism – including by entering voluntarily into labour service – might be forced to do so. The mix of humanitarian inclusivism and hard-edged utilitarianism was exemplified by the mid-century governorship of Sir George Grey, who proved eager to extend the benefits of civilisation to all but remained fully prepared to impose civilised values on recalcitrant barbarous peoples. The presumption that all races had similar potential for achievement went together with a view of the universality of Christian civilisation that had little or no tolerance for cultural relativism. Rights of citizenship, in other words, would only be recognised if colonised peoples renounced customs and cultural traditions considered anathema to progress and civilisation.

Claims for common citizenship based upon the potential similarity of humans everywhere engendered a counter-reaction which was frequently couched in the visceral language of essential biological difference. The rapid spread of scientific racist theory from mid-century led to a broad questioning of the possibility that all peoples were capable of ascending the scale of civilisation. This was amply clear in the vociferous brand of anti-humanitarian settler discourse found in publications and newspapers like Robert Godlonton's *Grahamstown Journal*. The British imperial strategy of unifying South Africa's diverse political units into a confederation implied that the liberal Cape would have to make concessions to the Boer republics (the South African Republic's *Grondwet* or constitution explicitly rejected 'equality in Church or State') and also to anglophone Natalians who shared with English-speaking counterparts in districts of the Cape midlands and Eastern Cape a deep antipathy to the 'humanitarian' lobby. The discovery of diamonds and gold in the interior during the 1870s and 1880s massively increased the demand for a large-scale, pliable migrant African workforce. All these factors combined to undermine standard liberal assumptions that political and social stability could be achieved by promoting the gradual emergence of a self-sufficient African peasantry.

Cecil John Rhodes, leading mining magnate and Premier of the Cape from 1890 to 1895, grasped this reality as clearly as anyone. For generations of white and black South Africans, his famous formulation of 'equal rights for all civilised men south of the Zambezi' stood as a definitive statement of meritocratic non-racial universalism. Yet, Rhodes really meant equal rights for *white* men,[42] and in this sense his pronouncement was a precursor of the later view (typified by Sir Alfred Milner) which assumed that imperial citizenship was coterminous with whiteness. Rhodes's actions as prime minister reveal that he was determined to constrain the growth of non-racial citizenship (in a manner analogous to the contemporaneous restriction of the rights of African Americans in the US South). In 1887, and again in 1892, measures were introduced to restrict Africans' access to the franchise, for example by excluding land held in communal tenure as a qualification for the vote. Attempts to restrict the franchise met with an immediate political response: the first explicitly political organisation to represent Africans, the Imbumba Yama Nyama, was formed at Port Elizabeth in 1882 to fight for 'national rights' (though in reality the organisation's reach was highly localised). Its name recalled the words of the early 19th-century visionary and Christian convert, Ntsikana, who had advised Africans to achieve 'unity that binds everyone together'.

Rhodes was also responsible for introducing the 1894 Glen Grey Act, the intention of which was to restrict land tenure and thereby force more Africans out to work as agricultural and industrial labourers. The Act also aimed to undermine the principle of direct political representation by introducing special 'councils' for Africans. Africans responded by creating Vigilance Associations to defend and in some cases to extend existing rights. On the question of voting, Rhodes made himself perfectly clear in 1894: 'we say that the natives are in a sense citizens, but not altogether citizens – they are still children … They are just emerging from barbarism. They have human minds and I would like them to devote themselves wholly to the local matters that surround them and appeal to them.'[43]

The shift from common citizenship to governance through communal institutions presaged by the 1894 legislation marked a significant move away from the liberal universalism associated with Governor Grey and the evangelical missionary tradition. Coupled with changes in the land tenure system and efforts to reduce blacks to units of labour, the Glen Grey Act anticipated the system of racial segregation that was introduced on a national basis in the first decades of the 20th century.

Unlike the Cape and Natal, the Boer republics

of the South African interior were governed by written constitutions. These rudimentary documents guaranteed rights for the burgher citizenry, who were responsible for electing the president and members of the legislature.[44] The Orange Free State's 'model' constitution of 1854 drew strongly on French and American examples. James Bryce, the noted Liberal historian and Oxford law professor, was greatly enamoured of the simplified republican constitution of the Orange Free State, wherein he 'discovered, in 1895, the kind of commonwealth which the fond fancy of the philosophers of the last century painted'.[45] This proud but rudimentary form of *volk* republicanism was determinedly racially exclusive and exhibited clear hostility to foreign – that is, British imperial – influence. Its championship of the rights of small states and nations (whose notion of freedom bears comparison with the Confederate states of the US) became a major animating ideology for Afrikaner nationalism in the 20th century. It is worth noting that when the apartheid government's Law Commission (1989) came out in surprise defence of a bill of rights, it made extensive reference to the republican tradition of the Orange Free State, praising its 'rigid' 1854 constitution as 'the first document in South Africa containing provisions of a human rights nature' and also for being a 'truly "autochthonous or home grown" bill'.[46]

The highly regarded Free State bench proved able to interpret the constitution and, on occasion, to reject proposals emanating from the Volksraad. By contrast, the constitution of the South African Republic (the Transvaal) lacked the clarity of its Free State equivalent. The relationship of the Volksraad to the Transvaal constitution was clouded in ambiguity and its provisions were therefore apt to be ignored.[47] Whereas the Orange Free State granted burgher status to all white males (with minimal residence requirements),[48] in the South African Republic the franchise entitlements of white immigrants to the goldfields became increasingly restrictive during the 1880s, though an agreement signed with the Orange Free State in 1897 granted reciprocal rights of citizenship to burghers emigrating from one republic to the other.

It was President Kruger's reluctance to grant full political rights to European immigrants and workers (*uitlanders*) that led the British High Commissioner, Sir Alfred Milner, to castigate the President of the South African Republic for treating British subjects as 'helots' or slaves – a primary *casus belli* in the lead-up to the South African (Boer) War in 1899. Many, if not most, *uitlanders* cared little for political rights in the South African Republic, yet anglophone *uitlanders* were invariably passionate in their assertion of their

Britishness. The presumption that subjects of the British empire, including its overseas working class, were entitled to special rights and privileges by virtue of being fellow colonial citizens of the white dominions was steadfastly defended. In this case, social rights and claims to special privileges were seen as racially coded benefits that followed from being a (white) subject of the British monarch.[49]

The use by British imperialists of a discourse of equal rights was castigated in *A Century of Wrong* (1900). This brilliant propaganda pamphlet, issued by F.W. Reitz, State Secretary of the South African Republic, was designed to puncture British illusions of moral rectitude by showing that it was Boers, not Britons, whose rights had been violated. The central argument sought to explode British hypocrisy in relation to what would today be termed 'humanitarian intervention'. 'History will show', the authors asserted, 'that the pleas of humanity, civilisation, and equal rights, upon which the British Government bases its actions, are nothing else but the recrudescence of that spirit of annexation and plunder which has at all times characterised its dealings with our people.'[50]

During the decade that followed the conclusion of the South African War, extraordinary efforts were made to create a common white South African identity shared by Afrikaners and English-speakers.

The inclusive white nation that was practically realised with the creation of the Union of South Africa in 1910 (a self-governing dominion within the British empire) was predicated on the exclusion of Africans, Coloureds and Indians as full citizens of the new nation-state. The 1910 political settlement also embraced Westminster-style precedents which were antithetical to the notion of a rigid written constitution or bill of rights – other than the 'protection' of existing franchise rights and equal language rights for Afrikaners and English-speakers.[51] This put paid to the 'traces' of the natural law tradition which had found expression in the 1854 constitution of the Orange Free State. In the neighbouring South African Republic, the 'testing' power of the judges – the judiciary's right to strike down or 'review' laws made by parliament – was effectively ended when Kruger overturned Judge Kotzé's bold attempt to reject legislation deemed to be contrary to its *Grondwet* or constitution. Kruger's dismissal of Kotzé in 1898 was widely condemned by Cape legal experts and it was cited by imperialists like Milner as further justification of the need to remove Kruger himself.

Neither Boer republicanism nor British constitutionalism (pace William Blackstone, whose *Commentaries on the Laws of England* proclaimed the sovereignty of parliament) disposed any of the major figures at Union to press for a 'rigid' constitution with a bill of rights.[52] This was to have important ramifications for the development of segregation in the unitary state of South Africa: successive governments found that parliamentary sovereignty was perfectly compatible with white supremacy. Neither the 1961 Republican constitution nor P.W. Botha's 1983 tricameral constitution accorded citizens fundamental rights. In fact, the 1983 'reforms', which purported to grant Coloureds and Indians equivalent citizenship rights to whites, merely highlighted the removal of Africans as South African citizens. It was only with the creation of a constitutional court in the second 'new' South Africa that judicial review – the testing right – has been instated and the relationship between parliament and the law significantly rebalanced. Yet, this remains a live point of contention. Welcoming the new Chief Justice, Mogoeng Mogoeng, at a special sitting of parliament on 1 November 2011, President Jacob Zuma warned that 'powers conferred on the courts cannot be regarded as superior to the powers resulting from a mandate given by the people in a popular vote'. President Kruger would no doubt have heartily agreed.[53]

5

Segregationism

In the period of post-war reconstruction (1902–10) and, even more, in the post-Union (1910–48) era, Afrikaners and English-speakers found common cause on the colour 'question'. The creation of the new South Africa as a white man's country entailed that blacks be subjected to unprecedented ideological and political scrutiny. Discussions about their moral and intellectual status, their capacity to absorb European civilisation and, indeed, the desirability of their being encouraged to do so, acquired urgency and focus as the 'Native Question' was constituted as a unitary problem requiring a national solution.[54]

The concept of segregation, which now entered general political discourse, was duly presented as the appropriate answer. Proponents of segregation assumed that the interests of blacks and whites were fundamentally at variance and they rationalised the need for political and social separation, either by reference to immutable racial differences or else on the theoretically more flexible grounds of cultural relativism. Considerable intellectual and political energy was expended in order to render Africans perpetual political minors by removing their vestigial citizenship and franchise rights. The old Cape notion that individual blacks might achieve citizenship rights through the Christian civilising process was eschewed by increasing numbers of whites, including many who thought of themselves as 'liberals'. It was increasingly assumed that a white skin conferred rights to minimum 'civilised' standards of pay and living conditions, and that 'non-whites' were second- or third-class citizens in perpetuity.[55]

Segregationist ideology presumed that Africans, being naturally suited to a 'tribal' existence, were best left to develop 'along their own lines' in specially delimited rural 'native reserves' – subject, of course, to their availability for labour on white-owned farms and in white industries. The elaborate system of labour migration that increasingly underpinned the South African economy helped to give practical reinforcement to the notion of 'tribalism', for it was to the tribal reserves that Africans returned after spells of labour service. Claims about the moral and practical value of tribal life entailed a decisive withdrawal from the 19th-century view that only by destroying tribal bonds and treating Africans as individuals could civilisation triumph over barbarity. In this process, the notion of the universality of natural rights on an individual basis yielded to a relativist understanding of collective cultural rights. (This would have ironic echoes, in the late 20th century, in claims by indigenous peoples and other self-defined constituencies with self-defined identities to secure *cultural* rights for *groups* rather than individuals.)

Although the scholarly literature on segregation has paid due attention to the loss of citizenship rights, it has tended to overlook the important fact that *South African* citizenship remained unspecified after 1910. The absence of a written constitution meant that there was no reliable guide to the question. Rights were defined as much by residual bonds of loyalty to the British Commonwealth or Crown as by membership of a new self-governing state. In the domains of law and administration, South African citizenship was largely defined negatively and tangentially, that is, in relation to attempts to control, register and naturalise immigrants, as well as in the process of classifying the population within strict racial hierarchies. At the 1911 Imperial Conference delegates strove to agree on a common imperial naturalisation policy, which, in effect, defined shared rights as belonging to empire citizens. A key question was whether a British subject *anywhere* should be a British subject *everywhere*.[56]

Strikingly, it was controversy over the use of Chinese indentured labourers (who were recruited to work on the gold mines in the immediate aftermath of the South African War and then sent back home after waves of hostile reaction) that led to the first concerted effort to exclude a defined racial group from potential citizenship (in 1904).[57] Indians were another non-indigenous group whose presence in South Africa served as a proxy for broader definitions of citizenship. The large-scale Indian presence in South Africa goes back to the 1860s when migrants were recruited as indentured labourers for the sugar plantations of Natal. In 1897 Natal passed an Immigration Restriction Act designed to exclude Indian immigrants by making competence in a 'European' language the basis for admissibility. (Although technically non-racial to get around constitutional objections relating to the rights of the Queen's subjects in India, the 'Natal Act' soon came to serve as a template for immigration restriction elsewhere in the empire, notably Australia and New Zealand, where Chinese were the principal 'Asiatic' targets.)[58] Indians' indeterminate status, both as South Africans and as British subjects, was taken up by the young lawyer M.K. Gandhi, who arrived in South Africa in 1893 and immediately began pressing for civic rights. Gandhi's technique of passive resistance (*satyagraha*) was essayed between 1906 and 1914 in numerous campaigns to do with residency and commercial and political freedoms. These brought him into direct conflict with the South African politician and statesman Jan Smuts, who, like Gandhi, was about to emerge as an advocate of freedoms and rights in the international arena.[59] Up to 1937 (when a more precise definition of 'Union nationality' was eventually arrived at in law) definitions of citizenship were thus shaped by the imperative to restrict the mobility and immigration of 'Asiatics'.[60] Though the admissibility of immigrants speaking a 'non-European language' was primarily targeted against Indians, it also affected 'unassimilable' Jews (Yiddish was only recognised as a European language after much pressure).[61]

Indigeneity provided some protection from the loss of South African citizenship, but not from the loss of attendant political rights. In the period leading up to the enactment of the 1936 segregation laws, the 'Hertzog Bills', Africans were increasingly denied civic and political rights, though their status as South Africans was not as yet affected. The core of the Smuts–Hertzog segregationist programme revolved around the idea of a historic compromise whereby the antecedent rights to land presumed by 'natives' were recognised in return for their loss of attendant franchise rights. This form of differential sovereignty bore down particularly heavily

49

on already enfranchised Africans resident in the Cape; they were stripped of their remaining citizenship rights in return for the promise that their compatriots elsewhere in the country could benefit from extended communal land rights in specified 'reserved' areas.

Leaving aside the flagrant inequities that this implied, our attention should be drawn to the manner in which Africans' political rights were to be sacrificed in return for promises of more land. Whereas the early 19th-century humanitarian missionaries and activists had insisted that legal and constitutional rights were essential to the provision of material and social rights, the novel inequity of 1936 was the assumption that one kind of right could be traded for another. Many liberals (black as well as white) were drawn into this dangerous discourse, often falling victim to the blandishments and flattery of politicians who sought out their opinions. Indeed, segregationists were explicit about the need to overturn the assumptions of 19th-century humanitarians and egalitarians whose outmoded views, it was argued, entailed that racial intermixture or 'assimilation' would inevitably occur in a common society without a colour bar.

Between 1910 and 1936 African and white opponents of segregation were increasingly pushed on the defensive. The ANC, founded in 1912, opposed segregation by reference to Rhodes's putative promise of 'equal rights for all civilised men'. There were also many appeals to the British monarch to recognise the loyalty that Africans had displayed in helping the empire to fight in the South African War and the First World War – loyalty being a demonstration of subject-citizenship. The ANC's pithy 'African Bill of Rights', adopted in 1923, cited Rhodes's dictum as one of several prongs in the claim to equal rights, along with being subjects of the King and the fact of natural descent in 'this land of their fathers'.[62] However, the ANC was weakened by a lack of consistent common purpose in respect of political rights and this was compounded by its own social elitism: only rarely did it speak for the masses of black people. The newspaper editor and ANC stalwart R.V. Selope Thema, who formed part of a 1919 ANC delegation to Britain and the League of Nations in defence of African rights, provides a typical example. In his pamphlet 'The Race Problem' (1922) Thema entreated: 'While we do not wish to encroach upon the society of the whites, nevertheless we claim our rights of citizenship first as the aboriginals of this country, and second as British subjects.'[63] By the early 1930s, Thema was one of those pressured defenders of the Cape franchise who were alleged to be prepared to do a deal with white segregationists.[64]

ANC leaders were not altogether estranged from the broader populace: the tendency of segregation to compress social gradations was a real source of anxiety for the African middle class. In some cases this parlous situation encouraged leaders to maintain ties with ordinary working-class Africans, whose political potential was considerable. In the mid-1920s, the ANC president Z.R. Mahabane remarked that if Africans were to be granted equal citizenship rights, then African workers would get 'satisfactory wages' and this would entail 'peace'. According to this logic, rights-based political claims would advance African nationalism as a whole, benefiting workers as well as the respectable African middle-class intelligentsia, and thereby discourage revolutionary tendencies.[65]

Other organisations, most notably the populist Industrial and Commercial Workers' Union (ICU), offered more radical mass-based opposition to segregation in the 1920s, resulting in hostile government reactions such as the sedition clause in the 1927 Native Administration Act. The social composition of the ICU meant that it was less concerned to defend common or individual rights than it was to resist everyday oppression of rural and urban workers. Its inspiring liberatory message, which was notably inflected by Garveyite ideas about racial solidarity, did not necessarily seek inclusion in a common society on the basis of equal citizenship. Rejectionism could be compatible with segregation if this was achieved on a more equitable basis. But by the end of the 1920s, the ICU had effectively collapsed. The depression era of the 1930s marked a nadir in African resistance, highlighted by the failure of the All-African Convention, a broad front opposition movement, to halt the imposition of segregation embodied in Hertzog's 1936 Acts.

The Second World War
and its aftermath

During the Second World War the ANC underwent revival as a mass-based organisation, its radicalism spearheaded by members of the newly constituted ANC Youth League, whose Johannesburg-based activists (including Anton Lembede, A.P. Mda, Walter Sisulu and Nelson Mandela) were increasingly prominent. During this era the rhetoric of African nationalism began to focus fully on the illegitimacy – rather than the unfairness – of white power, and on the necessity of replacing minority with majority rule. In conjunction with rights-based rather than rights-conditional approaches to citizenship, such thinking signalled a major change in expectations and entitlement. Whereas African nationalist leaders had routinely petitioned the Queen or King in their capacity as subjects of the monarchy until after the First World War (the phrase 'we humbly submit' was often employed by delegations), the Second World War soon put an end to such deferential discourse.

The emergence of mass-based politics, a growing international discourse of democratic rights and freedoms, and a developing anti-colonial sentiment in Africa and Asia, all helped to entrench the idea that to be an African was *ipso facto* to be a South African citizen, and that certain fundamental rights flowed directly from this status. This was a worldwide phenomenon. As Lake and Reynolds point out, the discussions that led to the United Nations and its Universal Declaration of Human Rights were framed 'not in terms of the equality of nations or races, as Japan had proposed twenty years earlier, but in the French and American traditions of the rights of individuals and the principle of non-discrimination, enunciated in 1929 by the Institut de Droit International'.[66]

Along with new ideas about democracy, words like 'welfare' and 'citizenship' became defining terms in the 1940s. The wartime reshaping of the ANC as a national organisation with a growing mass base (incorporating social democratic, communist and Africanist ideas) can be seen in key documents such as *Africans' Claims in South Africa* (including *The Atlantic Charter from the Standpoint of Africans*), which was adopted by acclaim as official ANC policy in 1943. The drafting committee was chaired by Professor Z.K. Matthews, whose intellectual imprint is clear in the document's espousal of democratic rights, citizenship, human dignity and anti-colonial national self-determination. *Africans' Claims* included a bill of rights, which began by demanding, as a matter of urgency, the granting of 'full citizenship rights such as are enjoyed by all Europeans in South Africa'.[67] As well as being the ANC's most ambitious and clear statement of African political aspirations and rights to date – including full adult suffrage – it is also notable for the way in which it genuinely universalised the meaning of freedom set out in the Atlantic Charter (rather against the wishes of Churchill, who immediately regretted that the phrase 'all the men in all the lands' in the Atlantic Charter might be taken as pertaining to the imperial context as well).[68] The document has been aptly characterised as 'a resolute assertion by Africans of their equal status in the community of humankind'.[69]

A recent (2005) effort by Kader Asmal and others to unify the tradition of human rights thinking in the ANC correctly identifies *Africans' Claims* as a foundational text but also argues, rather implausibly, that the document 'refutes any claim that the very idea of human rights was inherited from Europe or North America'.[70] The wartime years formed a moment in South Africa when international progressive (as well as fascist) ideas were circulating with unprecedented speed.[71] New approaches to rights, citizenship and nationhood were everywhere in the air and the Atlantic Charter resonated in many parts of the colonial world, Africa included. In Nigeria, for instance, the nationalist leader and editor Nnamdi Azikiwe took up the Charter in his Lagos newspaper, *The West African Pilot*. In 1943 he and other journalists presented the British Colonial Office with a memorandum, *The Atlantic Charter and British West Africa*, which called for Nigerian independence.[72]

During the 1940s long-standing transatlantic links were reaffirmed with African Americans by the ANC president Alfred B. Xuma, who forged a political alliance with the American pan-Africanist-inclined Council on African Affairs, led by Paul Robeson and Max Yergan. The Council on African Affairs looked to support the transatlantic African diaspora and 'international anti-colonialism'.[73] It was with the overt support of this radical organisation that Xuma petitioned the newly created United Nations in order to challenge Smuts's domestic racial policies – just as Smuts was inserting the very concept of 'human rights' into the preamble of the UN Charter, to great acclaim. The United Nations also pressed the Smuts government on its treatment of South West Africa (Namibia), which had been entrusted to South Africa under the mandates system of the League of Nations.

For anti-apartheid activists like the Anglican priest Michael Scott, South West Africa offered a means to criticise the apartheid regime at a time when the South African government's refusal to countenance attacks on its sovereignty (with reference to article 2/7 of the UN Charter concerning domestic jurisdiction) was proving difficult to overcome. Scott was also a key figure in the 1940s Campaign for Right and Justice, a broadly based South African pressure group that formulated in 1943 a 'Charter of Rights' whose stress on social justice drew directly on the principles of the Atlantic Charter. This manifesto bears close comparison with the contemporaneous bill of rights outlined in *Africans' Claims*.[74]

Smuts's introduction of the concept of human rights into the UN Charter was possible because of his eminence as an international statesman, his championship of the British Commonwealth, the direct link he represented with the League of Nations – and his contradictory views on freedom and rights in 'civilised' countries and at home. His refusal to countenance rights within South Africa has long marked him out as a hypocrite, but in this he was not alone. Mark Mazower has shown that the acceptance of human rights at this moment was significantly conditioned by a cynical belief among the great powers that it would have little practical effect – and that individual rights were in any case preferable to the system of ethnic 'minority rights' that had proved so problematic for the League.[75] Smuts rejected the modern idea of human rights as a universal claim, certainly if this implied egalitarianism or political equality for colonial subjects. He remained true to the opinion, which he had expressed with clarity forty years before, that politics was not for 'natives'.[76] In Smuts's conception, human rights referred to certain minimal requirements for life; they were also associated with individual and collective spiritual growth or evolutionary progress. He therefore preferred to think of rights as an 'organic' concept linked, on the one hand, to human dignity or personhood, and to notions of social unity, on the other. Crucially, rights were not entitlements. They had to be earned, and they were inextricably connected with obligations and duties.[77]

Smuts certainly did not intend that his concept of freedom, applicable to mature countries and cultures such as Europe, should affect the domestic situation of South Africa. Throughout his life he remained a staunch believer in white supremacy or, as he and many other whites would have it, a racial order based on Christian 'trusteeship'. According to this conception, relations between whites and blacks were bound by mutual ties of obligations and duties. In South Africa's variant of Kipling's 'white man's burden', whites were thus responsible for the gradual upliftment of backward people, who were obliged to serve as subjects, not citizens.

During the war years, greater recognition of the facts of interracial social and economic interdependence prompted reformists in Smuts's United Party to recognise the permanency of blacks in towns and cities. In this context Smuts showed some preparedness to entertain the extension of welfare benefits to black as well as white South Africans, albeit within the framework of a differential, racially coded rights regime that was explicitly anti-egalitarian. Liberal social democrats and more progressive thinkers within Smuts's government were certainly attuned to welfarist ideas of 'social citizenship', a concept foreshadowed by the Beveridge Report in Britain and formalised at the end of the decade in T.H. Marshall's classic essay on 'Citizenship and Social Class', which developed the concept of social rights out of existing British ideas around civil and political citizenship.[78] In South Africa, ideas of a broad-based social citizenship began to take root in fields such as health, nutrition and education from the late 1930s.[79] Radical thinkers may have hoped that such rights would pave the way for political freedoms and equality. But Smuts and other reform-minded conservatives regarded social welfare measures for blacks as a means of avoiding or deferring substantial political concessions.

By the 1940s the ANC increasingly refused to tolerate concessions in the sphere of welfare as a substitute for civic or political rights. Inspired by the worldwide democratic fight against fascism, young ANC intellectuals demanded citizenship rights as an entitlement rooted in South African nationality, birth and belonging. No longer could citizenship rights be offered by the colonial state as a reward for demonstrable cultural assimilation to standards of Western Christian 'civilisation', as had been the case in the 19th century, nor could they be traded for land and trusteeship, as the segregationist compact of the 1930s had required. When, in 1946, relations between the moderate Natives' Representative Council and the government broke down, councillors and the ANC made it clear that full citizenship rights and representation were the central issue, and no amount of 'benefits' would compensate. Recalling this episode, Z.K. Matthews made the point that in civilised and industrialised countries social 'benefits' were themselves regarded as 'rights'.[80]

In the case of the 1946–8 Indian passive resistance campaign against the Smuts government's 'Ghetto Act', a new generation of radicalised activists foregrounded claims to citizenship in ways that shifted the emphasis from Gandhian notions of moral 'truth' to the equally universalist – but more socially inclusive – language of democratic rights, equality and dignity. This concern echoed, in the domestic context, the dramatic struggle between India and South Africa that was then being played out in the international councils of the United Nations, while also signalling growing convergence with campaigns led by the ANC and Communist Party. The Transvaal Indian Congress president and Communist Party leader, Yusuf Dadoo, spoke in 1947 of the need for active cooperation between all the oppressed peoples in pursuit of 'basic human rights'.[81] Together with Monty Naicker and A.B. Xuma, Dadoo was a signatory to the historic 'Doctors' Pact' of the same year.[82] This statement of cooperation between the Indian and African National Congresses 'and other democratic forces' (including trade unions and communists) sought 'the attainment of basic human rights and full citizenship for all sections of the South African people'. Widely seen as a precursor to the Freedom Charter, the Doctors' Pact was a bold social democratic declaration whose anti-discriminatory rhetoric was frankly rights-based and geared towards conformity with the UN Charter. In many ways, it marks the high point of 1940s 'united front' social democracy and internationalism in South Africa.

7

Anti-apartheid

The Afrikaner nationalist government which came to power in 1948 on the promise to bring about 'apartheid' (though its meaning was as yet by no means clear) successfully preyed on white fears that Smuts's party contained closet liberals and that any concessions to blacks would result in the calamity of racial intermixture. The new regime duly embarked on a major legislative programme designed to entrench segregation. In response, the ANC launched ongoing campaigns of mass civil disobedience in order to resist apartheid's 'unjust laws', including restrictions on blacks' freedom of movement, residency, citizenship and political rights. A Joint Planning Council of the ANC and Indian Congress, which met in November 1951 to map out a programme of direct action and non-cooperation, stated as a 'fundamental principle' of the freedom struggle: 'Full democratic rights with direct say in the affairs of the Government are the inalienable rights of every individual – a right which in South Africa must be realised now if South Africa is to be saved from social chaos and tyranny and from the evils arising out of the existing denial of franchise rights to vast masses of the population on the grounds of race and colour.'[83]

Walter Sisulu followed this up in January 1952 with a letter (co-signed by the ANC president James Moroka) to Prime Minister D.F. Malan, notifying the government of the ANC's intention to campaign against the country's unjust laws. He recorded that the government 'continues to insult and degrade the African people by depriving them of fundamental human rights enjoyed in all democratic communities'. The reply by Malan's private secretary took issue with this point and gave voice to an explanation based on biological race determinism: 'I think, that it is self-contradictory to claim as an inherent right of the Bantu who differ in many ways from the Europeans that they should be regarded as not different, especially when it is borne in mind that these differences are permanent and not man-made. If this is a matter of indifference to you and if you do not value your racial characteristics, you cannot in any case dispute the European's right, which in this case is definitely an inherent right, to take the opposite view and to adopt the necessary measures to preserve their identity as a separate community.'[84]

This intractable response was diametrically opposed to the firm but reasonable tone of Sisulu's letter, whose references to constitutionalism and non-racism were beginning to sound time-worn. From within the ANC, liberal-democratic human rights discourse was being challenged from two directions. Radical Africanists, vocal in the ANC's influential Youth League, rejected the ethos of 'non-racism' that seemed to give disproportionate political weight to whites, Coloureds and Indians, especially those associated with the Communist Party. These tensions ultimately led to a split in the ANC and the formation in 1959 of the Pan Africanist Congress, whose views were closely attuned to those of decolonising Africa. From the left, the Communist Party was also disdainful of the language of human rights, especially if this connoted a form of bourgeois constitutionalism that neglected the primacy of class-based oppression. Heavily influenced by Stalinist thinking on the 'national question', while at the same time fixated by the 'uniqueness' of South Africa's oppressive system, communists began to debate the idea of 'internal colonialism' or 'colonialism of a special type'. This doctrine came to be reformulated in the thesis that the 'national democratic revolution' (that is, African nationalism) should be supported as a precondition for the emergence of revolutionary socialism. In this way communists could justify their entry into an alliance with the forces of African nationalism (the ANC).[85]

At the historic Congress of the People in 1955, the ANC was confirmed as first among equals within a liberation movement that was now structured as a parallel organisational alliance comprising interest groups (trade unionists and women) and peoples (African, Coloured, Indian and white). The radical tone of the Freedom Charter, which was adopted at this Congress, signalled a departure from the wartime aspirations of the ANC, which had laid such stress on blacks as equal citizens and equal human beings. Although the ANC's national conference in December 1954 had envisaged the Freedom Charter as 'the South African people's declaration of human rights', this formulation was played down as the Charter took shape. Increasingly, the theory of 'national democratic revolution' came to be expressed in tones of vernacular populism: the people, the masses, workers, peasants, and so on. Every constituent organisation at the Congress of the People bore the name 'South African' in its title, thereby reinforcing the idea that the Congress movement's goal was a unitary state in which 'national' and 'cultural' differences would be accorded recognition, even celebrated, so long as this did not jeopardise the achievement of a common or supra-South African nationality. This was made clear by Congress's strong disdain for 'tribalism' – a form of ethnic division which the ANC had sought to transcend since its inception, and which was now being actively promoted by the divide-and-rule policies of the apartheid government.

The quest for a shared South African identity was powerfully reiterated by the Freedom Charter's bold declaration (which the vocal Africanist constituency strongly contested) that 'South Africa belongs to all who live in it, Black and White' and the promise that 'all national groups shall have equal rights'. A notable inclusion was the claim for women's rights, a clear reference to the comprehensive demands for full gender equality and rights in the Women's Charter adopted a year previously at the inaugural gathering of the Federation of South African Women (Fedsaw). Yet, while affirming the shared community of interests of men and women in a single society, the Women's Charter claimed that many of 'our menfolk' were complicit in keeping women in a position of inferiority and subordination by refusing to 'concede to us women the rights and privileges which they demand for themselves'.[86] It was a pointed criticism, which anticipated the merely glancing attention accorded to women's demands in the Charter, and continued to reverberate as an issue of concern in Alliance politics.

Much of the controversy surrounding the Freedom

Charter at the time, and since, has focused on the question of whether it envisions a future non-racial social democracy or, alternatively, whether it should be read as a barely disguised socialist programme clothed in 'popular front' language.[87] Thus, while ambiguities in the so-called 'nationalisation clause' have been extensively debated, relatively little discussion has taken place on the mechanisms by which freedoms and rights are to be attained and maintained. This lack of clarity became a live issue in the 1980s as the liberation movement's attention turned to constitution-writing. It was also a matter of concern in the lead-up to the process of formulating the Charter.

It is generally accepted that the proposal for a 'Freedom Charter for the democratic South Africa of the future' was inspired by Z.K. Matthews, the distinguished Fort Hare academic and liberal-minded elder statesman of the Congress movement. Matthews suggested a 'national convention' or 'congress of the people' to the Cape ANC in 1953, judging that the phase of mass defiance had run its course. A fresh approach was now required in order to seize the political initiative. The principle of 'equal rights for all' underpinned Matthews's proposal.[88] It was also evident later that year when the ANC's annual conference called for a meeting of all democratic organisations subscribing to the principle of 'full citizenship rights for all'. Matthews was invited by the ANC president Albert Luthuli to work up his proposal in more detail. His memorandum envisaged that the process of mobilisation and idea-gathering should be tied to the creation of a common voters' roll with constituency-based elections, thereby approximating an alternative parliament or constituent assembly.[89] This was rejected as unworkable. Moreover, in proposing what might be interpreted as an alternative parliament, it ran the risk of being seen as treasonable. Instead, the National Action Council (to which Matthews was not elected) decided to elicit the demands of the people by means of door-to-door canvassing and mass meetings led by 'Freedom Volunteers'.

Lionel 'Rusty' Bernstein, loyal communist intellectual and future Rivonia triallist, notes in his autobiography that Matthews 'had proposed something new without intending to cause a revolution. But that was what happened. Relationships between Congress and the people had to be turned on their head; the people had to be encouraged to speak for themselves, and for the first time Congress activists had to learn to listen.' He regards it as paradoxical that 'the first outlines of a revolutionary new South Africa' were 'triggered by the most conventional, respectable, and thoroughly bourgeois activist of us all, Z.K. Matthews'.[90]

Others complained that the Charter, presented as an organic statement of ordinary people's wishes, was in fact authored by a small committee dominated by white Marxists from the Congress of Democrats.[91] Matthews himself stated that he was 'not dissatisfied with the manner in which the C.O.P. [Congress of the People] was carried out', but added that his 'fears that the meeting would be too big for detailed discussion were realised'.[92] Neither Matthews nor Luthuli was present at the Congress of the People (the former pleaded university business, the latter was ill and under a banning order) and neither was shown the draft of the Freedom Charter before its consideration at Kliptown.[93] Both leaders were forthright believers in constitutionalism and rights, and sceptical about the turn to armed struggle. Ongoing debate and strenuous resistance by the Africanists meant that the ANC was unable to adopt the Charter as its formal policy at its national conference in 1955 and decided to do so only the following year.

The Freedom Charter contains a clause stating that 'All Shall Enjoy Equal Human Rights!' and the word 'rights' recurs several times. But, even allowing for the aspirational tone in which it is written, there is no clear suggestion as to how such rights are to be protected or entrenched. Citizenship is mentioned only once and democracy is conceived in the radical idiom of popular sovereignty and collective 'will' rather than through the discourse of constitutionalism, which strongly informs Matthews's conception of the Charter and which is also to the fore in *Africans' Claims* and the Doctors' Pact. The Freedom Charter states that everyone should have the right to vote for all law-making bodies, but makes no mention of 'the Parliament of our land', as was the case in an earlier draft, or of the need for ongoing consultation between the people and their representatives. Whereas the draft Charter was to begin with a 'general clause of rights', this was lost in the Charter as adopted.[94] The demand for 'equal rights' in the Freedom Charter is positioned in relation to the equality of 'national groups' or in the context of the need to revoke apartheid laws. Human rights are therefore implicitly collectivised or nationalised in the Freedom Charter – in contradistinction to their usage in the UN Universal Declaration of 1948.

Conversely, the Freedom Charter is replete with claims to second-order social rights, including a share of the national wealth, land distribution, as well as access to housing, medical care, work, and so on. The Freedom Charter's ambitions are therefore oriented towards enhanced substantive rather than procedural rights. In neither case does the Freedom Charter specify how such rights are to be enforced (for example, by reference to a bill of rights or a constitution) other than by ill-specified 'democratic organs of self-government', a tell-tale Marxist-Leninist formulation of the time. This marked a significant shift away from the demands for 'equal rights' that featured so prominently in ANC documents from the 1940s; it also set the liberation movement on a very different course from the emerging civil rights movement in the United States. The Leninist principle of 'democratic centralism' was rapidly gaining ground.

Widespread suspicions that the Freedom Charter was a stalking horse for communism persuaded the Liberal Party to withhold its support and, more seriously, for Pan Africanists to split away from the ANC in 1958–9.[95] The banning and exile of the liberation movements in 1960 coincided with decolonisation and the sharpening of the Cold War. Pan Africanists placed emphasis on rights flowing from a common African identity (rather than the rights that could be claimed by all South Africans sharing common citizenship); while Marxist theoreticians within the ANC treated human rights with suspicion as coterminous with the bourgeois freedoms that underwrote class oppression. Hostility to liberal ideology therefore meant that politics pursued in the name of common citizenship or equal rights could be dismissed as irrelevant to the 'real' struggle, or even as a covert defence of the social inequities inherent in free-market societies.[96]

8

· Internationalising rights

International condemnation of apartheid was led by the United Nations. At the very first meeting of the General Assembly in 1946 strong criticism was registered at South Africa's treatment of its Indian citizens. The dramatic confrontation between Mrs Vijaya Lakshmi Pandit and General Smuts signalled the ebbing authority of the old Commonwealth and the rising power of soon-to-be independent India.[97] Consistent criticisms of South Africa's governance of South West Africa and of apartheid policies as presenting a danger to international peace and security served as further means to circumvent legal objections that the United Nations was not competent to intervene in a sovereign country's internal policies.[98] Crucially, the singularity of South Africa's racial policies came to serve as a key test of the United Nations' commitment to the universality of human rights and of the organisation's ability to provide international moral leadership.[99]

A specially constituted UN Commission found in 1953 that the policies of apartheid contravened the principles and spirit of the UN Charter and its preamble. It concluded that 'the doctrine of racial superiority on which the apartheid policy is based is scientifically false and extremely dangerous to internal peace and international relations ... [and] contrary to "the dignity and worth of the human person"'. In singling out domestic apartheid practices an important threshold of permissible diplomatic criticism was on the verge of being crossed.[100] After the 1960 Sharpeville massacre, the 'policies of apartheid' began to feature in the General Assembly as a central, stand-alone issue, occasioning (almost) unanimous condemnation.[101] In 1967 a General Assembly resolution affirmed the legitimacy of the struggle for human rights and fundamental freedoms in South Africa. And in 1973 the General Assembly adopted the 'International Convention on the Suppression and Punishment of the Crime of Apartheid', with its own reporting and trial procedures. The standard response by the South African government was to reject UN claims around human rights as part of an international communist onslaught and to insist on its right to internal jurisdiction over national policies. But it was not entirely immune from such criticisms.[102]

In the United States, the influence of the civil

rights movement was strongly felt, especially as a result of campaigns by the New York-based American Committee on Africa (ACOA), which emerged under the leadership of George M. Houser to give support to the ANC's Defiance Campaign.[103] From its inception in 1953, ACOA and its Africa Fund sought to influence the United Nations, frequently using the occasion of the annual UN-sponsored Human Rights Day in December to protest against apartheid repression in South Africa (sometimes with reciprocal support from organisations within South Africa).[104] ACOA's readiness to campaign against South Africa contrasts with the response of mainstream organisations like the NAACP, which, under strong pressure from the anti-communist American right in the early 1950s, retreated from support of 'human rights' and anti-colonialism to a more acceptable domestic vision of civil rights for African Americans.[105] In 1957 a 'Declaration of Conscience' (led by Eleanor Roosevelt and co-sponsored by the ANC president Albert Luthuli and Martin Luther King, Jr.) was timed to coincide with Human Rights Day. It condemned the 'organized inhumanity' of apartheid and called on South Africa to honour its obligations under the UN Declaration of Human Rights. Supportive demonstrations were held in Johannesburg and Cape Town, organised by senior churchmen and civil rights activists.[106]

In Britain, the anti-apartheid movement, which emerged in the early 1960s, was a broad coalition that made frequent reference to crimes against humanity perpetrated by the South African state and its callous disregard of fundamental human rights. Churchmen like Canon John Collins, Michael Scott and Trevor Huddleston all played a major role in establishing the AAM. They brought to the movement a strong tradition of Christian humanitarian ethics which connected back to the emancipationist movement of the early 19th century and highlighted apartheid as an affront to human rights.[107] In 1968 the British newsletter *Anti-Apartheid News* prepared a series of articles which contrasted the UN Declaration of Human Rights with the situation in South Africa. Oliver Tambo, who in exile did much to incubate the ANC's Christian moral tradition of Albert Luthuli, commemorated the 20th anniversary of the UN Declaration, by noting that 'South Africa has the distinction of being the only country in the world which boldly and unashamedly' contravenes the Declaration 'as part of its avowed policy'.[108]

Over the years, *Anti-Apartheid News* returned to the issue of human rights, yet this was never foremost in its campaign literature, largely because of the influence of activists who preferred to emphasise apartheid's relationship to capitalism. As one of the newly emergent global 'social movements', anti-apartheid agitation drew strongly on the rhetoric of human rights from the 1960s. Yet, this discourse was only one in a flexible repertoire (including anti-colonialism, anti-racism and anti-capitalism) whose deployment was governed by specific political contexts and oppositional cultures in which the Cold War loomed large.[109] Following Sharpeville, apartheid became a global metonym for the racially motivated abuse of human rights. The internationalisation of apartheid's iniquities thereby gave fresh currency to worldwide human rights awareness.

By way of reaction, the apartheid government burnished the Boer republican tradition of minority or communal rights, culminating in the Republican referendum of 1960 and South Africa's departure from the Commonwealth a year later. Afrikaner nationalism remained implacably hostile to the liberal 'humanist' emphasis on individual rights, convinced that these were a cipher for communism. Moreover, Afrikaner nationalism's radical nationalist traditions often failed to distinguish between communism and liberal humanism: both threatened the sovereignty of God whose will was expressed through his 'chosen' people. Conservative Afrikaner churchmen and theologians were especially irked by enemies like the World Council of Churches. In the field of jurisprudence, successive apartheid governments insisted that 'humanist' emphases on rights were inimical to the Calvinist foundations of the state.[110] Christian-nationalist philosophy, which provided the ideological backing for apartheid theory, was founded on a conception of cultural, ethnic, minority or 'group' – rather than individual – rights. In a major explication of the core principles of apartheid, the Secretary of Bantu Administration, Werner Eiselen (an academic anthropologist), specifically took issue with the concept of 'Human Rights' which was 'perpetually appealed to by our critics'. As one of Verwoerd's leading ideologists, Eiselen's response was that the proposed self-governing Bantustans would offer full national rights for Africans within their own cultural communities in ethnically defined homelands. Common citizenship and a universal franchise were therefore explicitly rejected.[111]

In the international arena human rights were increasingly viewed by South Africa's leaders as a tool in the hands of its enemies. America, leader of the so-called free world, was notably at fault – a criticism the government shared with the liberation movement. An apartheid educationist warned in 1966 that 'Americanism constituted a greater threat to the South African way of life and education than Communism' because the United States was so influenced by the culture of human rights.[112] This perception hardened a decade later when the Carter administration attempted, with considerable publicity, some sincerity but little success, to apply its new human rights policy to South Africa.[113] White national (and Afrikaner cultural) survival, the government countered, was itself a human right – a point that featured prominently in the 1977 general election.[114]

Only within the beleaguered circles of the liberal opposition and the legal profession was there any consistent talk of citizenship, constitutionalism or the need for a bill of rights guaranteeing substantive freedoms and liberties for all South Africans irrespective of colour. Yet, such rights were discussed almost entirely within the context of apartheid's denial of basic freedoms and they did not extend to economic or social expectations. A Civil Rights League was established in Cape Town in 1948, its paid-up membership (some 400) consisting mainly of white English-speaking academics and professionals. From 1958 the small organisation began a tradition of organising an annual public lecture to mark international Human Rights Day on 10 December.[115] The National Union of South African Students (Nusas) determined in 1957 that education could be democratic only in a democratic society founded on the UN Declaration of Human Rights.[116] A large and broadly representative 'Multiracial Conference' held in 1957 at the Wits Great Hall (which included participation and support from the Liberal Party and Congress leaders like Luthuli, Dadoo, Mahabane and Matthews) adopted the principle of a bill of rights as an integral element of a written constitution, coupled with universal adult suffrage.[117] A Cape-based group calling itself the South African National Convention Movement sought, in 1961, to draft a new constitution, representative of all the people of South Africa, that would incorporate a 'Bill of Rights'.[118]

The newly formed Progressive Party, which split away from the United Party in 1959 and which was less committed to non-racialism than the Liberals, attempted without even a remote hope of success to have a bill of rights included in the 1961 Republican constitution. It continued to press the concept – again without success – in debates around the 1983 tricameral constitution, introduced by P.W. Botha as part of his package of 'reforms'.[119] Caught between two powerful nationalisms, liberals of various tendencies remained internally divided as to the relative importance of narrowly defined civil or broader social rights, with many holding on to the view that political rights required a proven ability to exercise them in accordance with the precepts of 'Western civilisation'. After its foundation the Progressive Party committed itself to a qualified franchise in line with the recommendations

82

of its Molteno Commission; it also adopted Donald Molteno's recommendation of a 'rigid' constitution with an entrenched bill of rights comprising 'basic rights and fundamental freedoms'.[120] Some saw this as a means of redressing the constitutional deficiencies of 1910 whereby South Africa emerged as a unitary state with a sovereign Westminster-style parliament but no written constitution.

One organisation that campaigned tirelessly on constitutional and human rights issues was the liberal Black Sash. Originally established by middle-class white women in 1955 to protest against the government's abuse of the constitution in disenfranchising Coloured voters, under the direction of Sheena Duncan the Sash significantly broadened its activities from the mid-1970s to address the social consequences of apartheid on the lives of African women and the poor.[121] The Sash adopted the UN Declaration of Human Rights in 1960, following this up in 1971 with a nine-clause Charter detailing rights which it saw as being fundamental to all women – noting that these were denied to black women in particular. This Charter was presented to parliament in the form of a petition by the lone Progressive Party MP, Helen Suzman.[122] As was the case with the 1954 Women's Charter, which preceded the Freedom Charter, the gendering of rights predated and conditioned their absorption into the mainstream of the liberation movement. The same was to happen in the late 1980s when the ANC adopted rights concerning women, children and the family (as well as homosexuality) into its constitutional proposals.[123]

From the mid-1970s a number of non-governmental public interest law organisations emerged to champion human rights. These included the Wits University Centre for Applied Legal Studies (est. 1978), whose first director, John Dugard, was a leading academic researcher in the field of human rights; the Legal Resources Centre (1978–9), which, under the direction of the human rights lawyer Arthur Chaskalson,[124] mounted direct challenges to apartheid legislation (such as the pass laws and the Group Areas Act); Lawyers for Human Rights (1979); and the Human Rights Commission (1988). It was out of the direct experience and debates of such organisations that ideas around legal rights as weapons of the weak took root in civic society. This empowering concept began to percolate more widely within the emergent mass democratic movement, notably among trade unionists who were involved in key debates at this time centring on the strategic advantages (and risks) in obtaining statutory recognition for unions. In the process concepts of democracy and rights were given practical as well as theoretical meaning.

Another important, and sometimes overlooked, source of human rights thinking in South Africa was the churches. Charles Villa-Vicencio's impressive treatise on human rights, *A Theology of Reconstruction* (1992), regards South Africa's struggle for human rights as nothing less than a contribution to global justice.[125] It reminds us of the long involvement of religious thinkers in relation to human rights, especially as this notion arises out of ideas of dignity and humanity. In 1978 Bishop Desmond Tutu succeeded in persuading the Lambeth Conference to commit the worldwide Anglican communion to give full support to those around the world 'fighting for human rights'.[126] His eventual successor as Archbishop of Cape Town, Winston Njongonkulu Ndungane, a former prisoner on Robben Island, completed a master's dissertation in theology at the University of London in 1979 in which he explored the relation between concepts of human rights and the Christian doctrine of man.[127] In the case of the Black Consciousness movement, which had strong connections with the Christian church and sought to recover a sense of common humanity and personal dignity, references to human rights flowed naturally out of concerns with the spiritual and religious dimensions of freedom. Yet, the concept of *individual* rights was not strongly developed here.

Theological influence was also clearly evident in the case of the law professor Johan van der Vyver, who left the conservative University of Potchefstroom in 1978 as a consequence of his ethical criticisms of apartheid. Arguing directly against the grain of received wisdom, and by reference to a wide range of international jurisprudence, Van der Vyver maintained that Calvinism was fully capable of deriving natural law and human rights from the word of God.[128] He also initiated a pioneering conference on the subject of human rights, held under the auspices of the University of Cape Town's law faculty in 1979, which attracted a large international audience.[129] In 1985 the *South African Journal of Human Rights* was formed to act as a specialist academic forum for the exchange of intellectual ideas and practitioner experience.[130] Another important contribution to specialist thought on human rights was the symposium on a bill of rights organised in 1986 by the law faculty at the University of Pretoria, then widely regarded as a bastion of conservative thinking. The conference attracted notable figures in the judiciary as well as leading law academics and opinion-formers. G.P.C. Kotzé, a retired Appeal Court judge, noted with dry understatement in his opening remarks that a bill of rights was 'a concept which many South Africans shrink from discussing'. To many, the conference signalled an awareness in legal and political circles of the major institutional changes that had to take place if the country was to return to political stability.[131]

9

The embrace of human rights

The efflorescence of human rights organisations in South Africa during the 1970s and 1980s was closely associated with the rise of civil society and non-governmental institutions. These anti-apartheid bodies tended to operate largely independently of mainstream (and banned) political organisations like the ANC, which, as we shall see, was itself beginning to work in parallel on constitutional and rights issues. Some anti-apartheid organisations within the country adopted human rights for pragmatic reasons, while others were fully committed to its core principles or became so over time. In the mid-1980s many such organisations became affiliated to the United Democratic Front (UDF), a broad-front civic and populist supra-body that helped to reintroduce ANC or 'Charterist' traditions into South Africa at a time of growing social crisis and open mass resistance.

At the opening meeting of the UDF in August

1983, Allan Boesak, a well-known Cape Town activist and preacher, swept the crowd into a rapturous call–response chant: 'We want all of our rights, we want them here, and we want them now!'[132] This invocation of 'rights', whose oratory and cadence consciously evoked the civil rights language of Martin Luther King, was primarily geared towards mass resistance. It also contained within it a strong claim to democratic political rights, not least because the UDF's formation was initially focused on opposition to P.W. Botha's tricameral constitution and the need for a national convention to fashion a constitution based on the 'will of the people'.[133] The rights rhetoric of the 1980s therefore operated at two levels, which were sometimes in tension with one another. In the first place, the discourse was oriented to the strategic recovery of political space in a country that was in the midst of a new phase of serious government repression. As such, the language of rights was deployed to delegitimise the regime and apartheid (long seen as a crime against humanity) as well as to defend individuals who suffered from abuses such as detention without trial, state-sponsored killings and torture during the successive states of emergency imposed from 1985 onwards. Secondly, the language of rights addressed concerns about the denial of citizenship and political freedoms and, in doing so, pointed to the urgent demand for a unitary South Africa based on non-racial, democratic principles. By referencing the Freedom Charter, the UDF recalled the more open and pluralist politics of the 1950s.[134]

Human rights awareness was also becoming more pervasive in the rapidly developing trade union movement, which, by the mid-1980s, was oriented as much towards broad social and political transformation as the furtherance of its members' workplace interests. Dunbar Moodie's analysis of the National Union of Mineworkers shows how, under the leadership of Cyril Ramaphosa, the union foregrounded demands for the recognition of human dignity – or workers' rights – so as to fundamentally challenge the racist underpinnings and dehumanisation of the industrial process.[135] The lived experience of campaigns against the violation of legal rights, coupled with a spirited assertion of racial equality (or non-racism), meant that concepts of rights gained currency for ordinary people involved in the anti-apartheid struggle.[136] Such ideas naturally gave prominence to claims to worker rights, including the right to strike, to engage in collective bargaining and to form trade unions, but they also extended much further into the political and civic domain. In 1989 the leading trade union consortium, Cosatu, resolved to adopt a Workers' Charter and in 1991 a Cosatu–ANC workshop was convened in Johannesburg on 'worker rights and the new constitution'.[137]

The internal struggle against apartheid during the 1980s saw increasing recourse to rights discourse in the context of popular demands for democracy, non-racism and social democracy. This ran parallel to, though it was not identical with, a growing awareness among some leading figures in the exiled ANC of the need to firm up its ideas about constitutional matters in the light of the possibility of political negotiations. In Lusaka, the ANC president Oliver Tambo recognised the need for the ANC to generate its own ideas, lest it be suddenly outflanked by government proposals or overseas initiatives like the Commonwealth Eminent Persons Group, which had tried (without success) to map out a scheme for negotiations in the first half of 1986. There was much talk in academic and policy circles during the 1980s about the prospects for confederation, consociationalism and other variants of 'power-sharing'. As a result of all this, an ANC Constitutional Committee was set up in January 1986, chaired by the sometime Communist Party intellectual Jack Simons, a renowned former University of Cape Town lecturer in comparative African government and law. The presence on the Constitutional Committee of Kader Asmal and Albie Sachs, both independent-minded academics with significant international experience, provided the ANC with creative intellectual resources.[138] This was all part of the process of projecting the ANC as a government-in-waiting.

The Constitutional Committee put its initial ideas to the ANC's National Executive Committee early in 1986.[139] It duly received an encouraging but 'very critical' reply from Ruth Mompati, noting that this was the first time that the ANC had 'even attempted to give constitutional expression to its programmatic demands'. (To Jack Simons's intense annoyance, the first drafts produced by his committee were rejected as being 'too bourgeois'.)[140] Among the problems raised by Mompati was whether the proposals were designed to be a 'mobilising instrument' or a 'tactical tool' in the event that 'negotiations are forced upon us'. She also pressed for recognition of gender rights. A further question was how to translate the slogan 'Power to the People' into a framework that was responsive to the masses. The Constitutional Committee had no ready answers to these questions, which raised fundamental problems in respect to popular legitimacy, process and strategy – at a time when the political context was in a state of rapid and uncertain ferment and the ANC was still rhetorically committed to the revolutionary seizure of power.[141]

As a result of its long history of diplomatic dealings with the United Nations and Western governments, some exiled leaders of the ANC were fully aware that to claim the mantle of human rights was a distinct advantage, not least because apartheid was widely regarded as embodying their denial. Yet, there were also serious disincentives to this course of action. Through most of the Cold War, official ANC propaganda had played down human rights discourse, especially if this was cast in terms of bourgeois individualism, gradual reform or liberal proceduralism. The United States' foreign policy agenda in Africa and Latin America – with its talk of democracy and human rights – rankled with a liberation movement that identified America as the centre of global imperialism.[142] Suspicion of the United States' real intentions in South Africa came to a head in the 1980s as Congress battled over whether to endorse mandatory sanctions. President Reagan, a firm opponent of sanctions and disinvestment, used the occasion of Human Rights Day in 1984 to condemn apartheid – but his change of rhetoric in criticising Pretoria satisfied no one. Even Edward Kennedy, who gave public support to the anti-apartheid movement during a high-profile visit he made to South Africa in 1985, drew strong criticism from radical organisations, who considered he might just as easily be a 'foe' as a 'friend'.[143]

There were good grounds for such scepticism. In his 1970 tour of Africa, William Rogers, Nixon's

Secretary of State, had declared: 'we take our stand on the side of those forces of fundamental human rights in Southern Africa as we do at home and elsewhere.'[144] Rogers's statement followed the signing of the Lusaka Manifesto by fourteen African states a year earlier. Endorsed as well by the Organisation of African Unity and the United Nations, this accord (which strongly endorsed the language of human rights and called for negotiations in southern Africa) was in part intended to constrain the ANC's armed wing, Umkhonto weSizwe (MK).[145] ANC opposition to the Lusaka Manifesto was conspicuously evident at the organisation's key consultative conference at Morogoro in 1969, which strongly reaffirmed the ANC's commitment to 'revolutionary armed struggle'. The South African government also rejected the Lusaka Manifesto, notwithstanding Prime Minister Vorster's experimental policy of 'détente' with compliant African neighbours. In the mid-1970s neither the liberation movement nor the South African government warmed to the Carter administration's human rights-based foreign policy. It was viewed by the government as part of a hostile international, communist-led campaign, and rejected by the ANC, which continued to place its faith in the armed struggle, revolutionary socialism and anti-imperialism. Both parties regarded American human rights initiatives as unwelcome interference and neither was persuaded by frequent parallels drawn by Carter and his diplomats with the American South and the civil rights movement.[146] If there was support for human rights in either constituency, such views were firmly in a minority.

Until the mid- to late 1980s, it is indeed difficult to discern a sustained interest in human rights within leading liberation movement organisations, other than when it was seen as politically advantageous for solidarity movements to invoke human rights discourse. One reason had to do with the human rights record of the ANC itself, which was vulnerable to claims that its security wing, *Mbokodo*, was responsible for torturing cadres accused of spying or participating in mutinies in guerrilla strongholds. Abuse was reported to have been rife in the ANC Quatro camp in Angola. These reports gave rise to unease within the ANC, strengthening the hand of those who considered that punishment, ranging from routine humiliation to summary execution, stemmed from a lack of judicial process. ANC figures with legal training and an interest in human rights took a lead – but they were evidently compromised by the nature of internal inquiries as well as the ethos of internal discipline and loyalty demanded by the movement.

At the ANC's consultative conference in Kabwe in 1985, a new 'Code of Conduct' was drawn up by

Albie Sachs and others. The ratification of the Code amounted to an acknowledgement of the need for demonstrable restraints on institutional power and of the rights of individuals within the ANC to procedural justice when accused of disciplinary breaches. Yet the Code was not enforced and, although Zola Skweyiya was appointed to the newly created post of Officer of Justice in 1986, he was prevented from visiting Quatro camp, where abuse of ANC cadres continued. Sachs chaired a 1990 ANC commission into the death of 'Thami Zulu', a senior MK commander in Natal who was, almost certainly, wrongly accused of being a government agent. There was speculation that Jacob Zuma, then head of counter-intelligence, might have been involved in poisoning Zulu immediately after his release. Though the commission found that Thami Zulu had not died directly as a result of his incarceration, Sachs attracted criticism for failing to consider the wider context of ANC prisoner abuse, even as he publicly embraced the cause of human rights and constitutionalism in articles and books.[147]

It is worth contrasting this episode with revelations within South Africa that Winnie Mandela's 'football club' was responsible for widespread thuggery, including the murder of a young activist, Stompie Moeketsi (Seipei). Murphy Morobe, speaking on behalf of the Mass Democratic Movement in 1989, frankly condemned Winnie and declared that the MDM was 'not prepared to remain silent where those who are violating human rights claim to do so in the name of the struggle against apartheid'.[148]

This forthright public declaration raised the wider issue of double standards in the application of human rights, a problem that emerged again when Kader Asmal, prominent ANC constitutionalist and human rights advocate, pointedly rejected any moral equivalence between government torturers and those employed by the liberation movement, following the publication in 1992 of an internal ANC commission of inquiry into the complaints of 32 of the ANC's detainees.[149] A similar line of argument recurred during the Truth and Reconciliation Commission hearings when ANC leaders insisted that crimes committed by those fighting against apartheid could never be equated to those committed in its defence. How was it, ANC supporters reasonably asked themselves, that some of the very same white politicians who had run the country in the apartheid era without the constraints of rights provisions were suddenly keen on constitutional checks and balances now that majority rule was in sight? It was also alleged that those in favour of a bill of rights – typically, (liberal) critics of apartheid – were not positioned at the 'heart' of the liberation struggle and therefore lacked credibility.[150]

There were other good reasons why human rights did not easily find favour in the ANC. The fact that some of the apartheid-created Bantustans (such as Bophuthatswana and Ciskei) sported incongruous bills of rights in their founding constitutions provided little by way of positive endorsement or legitimacy.[151] The ANC was certainly also not encouraged by the much trumpeted KwaZulu-Natal Indaba of 1986, which included a comprehensive bill of rights as part of a federal constitutional package that involved governing the region through a form of multi-racial consociationalism. Together with the UDF, it flatly rejected the exercise (not least because of the close involvement of Mangosuthu Buthelezi's Inkatha movement) as a further step towards the balkanisation of South Africa. Kader Asmal specifically criticised the rights provisions as a mechanism for 'privatising apartheid'.[152]

The formation of the anti-apartheid UDF, and the reassertion of the (African National) Congress tradition which accompanied it, led to a significant revival of interest in the iconic thirty-year-old Freedom Charter. There was much debate at this time around the document's socio-economic intent: in short, whether it should be read as supportive of state socialism or of liberal or social democracy. These debates occluded precise discussion about how the constitutional and legal rights of 'the people' would be protected – beyond the presumption that non-racism should be a cardinal principle and that all who lived in South Africa should share in South African citizenship. Fully thirty years elapsed between the production of the Freedom Charter and the 1987 decision by the ANC National Executive Committee to endorse the idea of a justiciable bill of rights based on fundamental rights and freedoms.[153] This novel idea was given further credence in the ANC's 1989 Harare Declaration, which included the clause 'All shall enjoy universally recognised human rights, freedoms and civil liberties, protected under an entrenched Bill of Rights'.[154]

Even as individuals within the ANC and the National Party edged their organisations towards the idea of a bill of rights, both sides remained wary of creating a body of law that allowed judges to review legislation passed by parliament – or, in other words, measures not under their own political control. When formal negotiations began between the government and the ANC over a solution to the South African political crisis, the former's determined invocation of ethnic 'group rights' was countered by the latter's proprietorial claim to represent 'the people' (always conceived of in the singular, as if to signal African primacy and indivisibility). Afrikaner and African nationalism thus shared elements of a common discourse, with the government emphasising ethnic or cultural rights, and the liberation movement stressing deliverance from 'national oppression'. Unlike the government, which now explored variants of federalism in order to protect white interests, the ANC insisted on majority rule in a unitary South Africa. This disposed it to think more precisely about citizenship and human rights, having up till now relied on the inspiring but unspecific guidance of the Freedom Charter.

In 1991 the first round of open political negotiations began with the Convention for a Democratic South Africa (Codesa), which brought together the government and ANC, as well as seventeen other political 'stakeholders', in an effort to hammer out a new political dispensation. Strikingly, the principle of a 'justiciable' bill of rights was one of the key areas of consensus in the process of establishing the constitutional principles of a 'new' South Africa. Yet, there remained a great gulf in terms of understanding what rights might entail and how they ought to be secured. The negotiations, conducted largely in secret, brought together a wide range of legal specialists and the bargaining process was a complex mixture of compromise and calculation which gave rise to unexpected alliances and surprising outcomes.[155] In this lengthy, disrupted and tumultuous process, fears voiced by those like Albie Sachs that deals would be done by experts behind closed doors gained credence. Yet it is likely that a bill of rights could be agreed only by experts working in relative secrecy. This is substantially what occurred.

The Codesa process broke down in 1992 amidst recriminations and heightened political violence. When it reconvened, in May 1993, as the Multi-Party Negotiating Process, seven non-partisan technical committees were created, one of which oversaw the drafting of an interim bill of rights. Four expert lawyers were charged with the detailed drafting of 'fundamental rights'.[156] One of these, the Cape Town law professor Hugh Corder, tellingly characterises the committee members collectively as 'partisan' defenders of the rule of law.[157]

Albeit loosely politically aligned, the negotiators were able to operate with a substantial degree of autonomy. This was partly because the process was insulated from public scrutiny. It was also a consequence of the pressing time constraints under which they operated. United States, Canadian and German models considerably influenced their detailed work, building on the earlier principles agreed at Codesa and the specific proposals of the government and ANC. They were also able to consult several locally produced contributions to the burgeoning rights debate, including the *Charter for Social Justice* produced by a group of progressive Cape-based lawyers, whose authors included Hugh Corder and Kate O'Regan (a future Constitutional Court judge).[158]

Other than the specific case of Namibia, whose liberation struggle had direct relevance to South Africa, wider African referents such as the African Charter on Human and Peoples' Rights (1981) were not major influences. The four lawyers worked on the principle of 'sufficient consensus', which effectively meant that their proposals had to be acceptable to the government, the ANC and the Inkatha Freedom Party (until the IFP left the process in mid-1993). Alongside the technical committee, an ad hoc committee composed mostly of political representatives was constituted to resolve contentious matters. Over time the two committees effectively merged and sat jointly, itself an indication of growing mutual trust and professional respect.[159]

The ANC favoured a 'minimalist' approach to the interim bill of rights, regarding the transitional phase of constitution-making as merely preparatory to a final constitution that would follow popular elections (in which its own leverage and legitimacy were certain to be enhanced); by contrast, the Democratic Party and the government sought to draft a more comprehensive 'maximalist' bill on the assumption that there was only a limited time to influence the negotiating process and therefore as much as possible should be secured during the as yet undefined period of political 'transition'. Yet, in deferring its full proposals till later, the ANC seems to have miscalculated and its direct influence in the transitional stage was accordingly diminished: the drafting committee took the view that 'the danger of protecting too few fundamental rights and freedoms during the transition was greater than that of protecting too many'.[160]

Though explicable in terms of political calculation, it is paradoxical that the liberation movement, with its strong commitment to egalitarianism, favoured a minimal approach, whereas the minority parties like the government and the Democratic Party adopted the fuller 'optimalist position'.[161] Whether the ANC erred tactically or whether its generally accommodating approach to this stage of the drafting process was deliberate strategy is difficult to determine. Not for the first time, the ANC found itself responding to, rather than leading, proposals on fundamental rights, on the grounds that the time was not yet right. Lack of internal organisational unanimity on the scope of justiciable rights in the new South Africa might have been a factor in staying the ANC's hand. Overconfidence in its capacity to control the process once in power may be another. It may even be the case that the ANC was beginning to realise that constraints on government increase in direct proportion to the breadth of constitutionally defined rights, as does the requirement of government to justify its actions and policies. Future historians may be better placed to answer these problems: they all have a bearing on our understanding of the ANC's current position on rights and constitutionalism.

Whatever the case, the consensus achieved by the negotiators on the interim bill of rights was remarkable, not only given the levels of political violence over the preceding decade, but also because the principal parties to the agreement remained far apart in public. Broadly speaking, the government favoured constitutional rights that would *limit* the powers of a future democratic government, while at the same time protecting 'minority' groups (like Afrikaners). By contrast, the ANC and other anti-apartheid parties took the view that any bill of rights in a democratic South Africa should actively advance the interests of those – in this case, the majority – who had suffered dispossession as a result of the country's long history of oppression.[162] The ANC was thus implacably opposed to the government's attempts to guarantee ethnic or racial 'group' rights. From the ANC's perspective, majority rule in a unitary South Africa could be most effectively advanced by supporting *individual* rights, subject to the endorsement of 'collective' rights where these pertained to socially defined constituencies (such as workers, women and children).[163] This placed it squarely within internationally accepted social democratic norms.

The government had already travelled a fair distance to reach the point where it was prepared to accept justiciable rights. Its willingness to do so was for many a tacit admission of growing weakness: the *Natal Mercury* greeted the National Party's Charter of Rights, unveiled in 1993, as a 'remarkable death-bed conversion'.[164] As has been noted, apartheid was predicated on the ontological primacy of groups, rather than individuals. Its flagship Bantustan policy, for instance, was a device for divide and rule that purported to turn the African majority into various ethnic 'minorities' while stripping them of South African citizenship: through this topsy-turvy process, the white (or Afrikaner) minority metamorphosed into a sovereign majority. The patent failure of this conjuring trick engendered an attempt, through the complex mechanisms of the 1983 tricameral constitution, to incorporate Indian and Coloured minority groups in an alliance with whites. But the collapse of these reforms made it clear to many, if not most, whites that the rights of the black majority could no longer be denied and that citizenship would have to be extended to all South Africans.

It was in this uncertain context that government-aligned intellectuals (with significant support from the judiciary) became more open to seeing individual constitutional rights and the rule of law as a prudent protection against a future government based on majority rule.[165] The government's receptiveness to human rights was sharpened by the prospect that a socialist regime might threaten the sanctity of private property and white vested interests. Rights, it was hoped, could be invoked to defend privileges without recourse to apartheid's racial mechanisms. Lawyers were not slow to realise that there was a legal platform to build upon, for the state's commitment to rule *by* law (though not rule *of* law) had remained relatively intact through the apartheid era, even surviving the suspension of judicial norms during the states of emergency of the 1980s. Moreover, the existence of a relatively unfettered press, notwithstanding bouts of censorship, managed to keep freedom of speech substantially alive. In both these aspects, South Africa was unlike many other transitional oppressive regimes in Africa, Latin America and Eastern Europe. For all that law had become grossly deformed under apartheid, strong traditions of *legality* still persisted. This 'not only facilitated South Africa's transition to democracy, but also provided an important foundation for the legal system in that democracy'.[166]

In 1986 the Minister of Justice, Kobie Coetsee,

instructed the government's statutory Law Commission to make recommendations about the definition and protection of group rights and – to the great surprise of the legal fraternity – consider the possible introduction of a bill of rights.[167] A working group under the direction of Justice P.J.J. Olivier was deputed to undertake the task and members of the general public as well as expert lawyers were invited to submit views. Some suspected that the Law Commission would use the opportunity to kill off the idea of a bill of rights or speculated that the initiative might be little more than a ruse to forestall American sanctions. Notwithstanding his conservative credentials, Olivier became converted to the concept of human rights in the process of thinking about them.[168] In 1989 the Commission duly produced a draft bill of rights which endorsed basic civic and political freedoms and firmly rejected the protection of racially defined group interests – while leaving the way open for the protection of cultural, religious or language rights.[169] Surprising as this was, it did not go entirely against the grain of reformist thinking. President Botha's opening address to parliament in 1986 stated that the government was committed to the 'sovereignty of law as the basis for the protection of the fundamental rights of individuals as well as groups'.

In a document circulated at the time by the

secretive elite Afrikaner Broederbond, entitled 'Basic Political Values for the Survival of the Afrikaner', the 'prerequisites of survival' were defined as, among others, the protection of language and cultural rights, private ownership, freedom of conscience and freedom of speech – all of which could in turn be described as 'basic human rights'.[170] But F.W. de Klerk, who became State President in September 1989, sidelined the Commission's findings and, together with Gerrit Viljoen, Minister of Constitutional Affairs, continued to press for power-sharing mechanisms rooted in group rights.[171] Claims for minority or group rights were, of course, by no means uniquely South African. Self-determination and protection for minorities had been an article of faith for the League of Nations and it was only after the demise of the League that its successor, the United Nations, adopted individual human rights. What made South Africa unusual was that the language of minority rights was deployed not as a *defence* against oppression by a majority, but as a means to *discriminate* against the majority. Now that continued racial discrimination was no longer feasible, the government was using the language of minority rights to preserve privileges gained as a result of centuries of dispossession.

At precisely the same time, the ANC was beginning to reconsider its own views. The ANC's draft bill of rights was composed by Asmal and Sachs on the former's kitchen table in Dublin, following Sachs's near assassination in Mozambique in 1988 by South African government agents.[172] In 1988, too, the ANC published its 'Constitutional Guidelines', which sought to translate the aspirations of the Freedom Charter into realisable constitutional principles. The Guidelines, which had been through multiple drafts since the Constitutional Committee began to deliberate in 1986, were discussed at an 'in-house' meeting in Lusaka in March 1988, attended by around fifty ANC officials and international representatives. The Guidelines affirmed the need for 'firm protection to the fundamental human rights of all citizens' and recommended the inclusion of a bill of rights in a future constitution.[173] Although said to have been inspired by the Freedom Charter, in practice the Guidelines went much further, not least by specifying basic rights, including those relating to property. They therefore represented a marked advancement in the ANC's acceptance of liberal-style political pluralism, while remaining guidelines rather than principles: a provisional steer into an uncertain future.[174]

Zola Skweyiya presented the ANC's ideas to a meeting in 1989 of ANC representatives and South African lawyers in Harare. He explained that the Guidelines stressed the need 'for the protection and extension of human rights to all and the redistribution of land', while completely rejecting 'the notion of "group rights"'. But, taking account of a continuing lack of unanimity within the ANC, as well as a tactical need to maintain flexibility in possible negotiations, Skweyiya emphasised that these were merely proposals and that a final constitution could only be arrived at by the elected representatives of all the people in a future parliament.[175] Likewise, Sachs took care to emphasise that rights could not be used as the basis for protecting entrenched privilege; they would only be acceptable if they amounted to an enlargement of freedoms, and this would not be secured by lawyers meeting behind closed doors. He frankly admitted the paradox that the demand for a bill of rights in South Africa emanated first from 'a certain stratum in the ranks of the oppressors', rather than from 'the ranks of the oppressed'. Such was the heightened level of suspicion towards the apartheid regime's constitutional reforms that some young black lawyers had actually organised an 'anti-bill-of-rights-committee'.[176]

In October 1990 the ANC's Legal and Constitutional Committee released its provisional draft bill of rights for discussion. Appearing before the final report of the South African Law Commission, and prior to official endorsement by the ANC's National Executive Committee, it was greeted by Nicholas Haysom of

Wits University's Centre for Applied Legal Studies as 'an opening salvo in the unfolding constitution-making process'. The document drew on international jurisprudence but also located itself as an indigenous product designed for all South Africans, which 'defends each and every one of us against the kinds of tyranny and abuse which have flowed daily from the apartheid state'.[177] While strongly affirming individual rather than 'group' rights, it nonetheless took account of cultural and language rights and also made explicit reference to the rights of sectoral groups such as women, homosexuals, workers and children. It attempted to combine elements of the 'shield' (protection of political and civil rights) with the 'sword' (duties incumbent on the state to provide social and economic security).

The circulation of an ANC discussion document, *Constitutional Principles and Structures for a Democratic South Africa* (1991), consolidated the movement's thinking about rights over the previous five years. Presented in clear and concise prose, it envisaged 'a united, democratic, non-racial and non-sexist South Africa, a unitary State where a Bill of Rights guarantees fundamental rights and freedoms for all on an equal basis'.[178]

Yet, even at the start of formal meetings with the government in 1991, ANC members of the Constitutional Committee had to work hard to reassure activists in the liberation movement that a rights-based constitution would not jeopardise the objectives of 'people's power' and revolutionary change. There had been much talk within the ANC of a 'people's power' constitution but no detailed explanation as to what this might mean. Rank-and-file ANC members had to be persuaded that constitutional rights were in the objective interests of the people. This necessitated a major shift in the cultural and intellectual mindset of the ANC and the Mass Democratic Movement. The flavour of such scepticism was clearly evident at a symposium on a bill of rights organised at the University of the Western Cape in 1988. The lawyer Yasmin Shehnaz Meer warned that 'a bill of rights could also, like all law, be simply a tool of the state to dominate subordinate classes and further the interests of the ruling class'; Dennis Davis asserted that it was impossible to conceive of a bill of rights in the context of the ongoing state of emergency and the existing security legislation; while Dullah Omar (who became Minister of Justice in 1994) declared that, although he was in favour of a new constitution, he was against a bill of rights because the political context was not conducive and individual rights should not be privileged over meaningful social and economic rights.[179] Omar restated his objections in 1993 in rejecting the government's proposed interim bill of human rights. Under conditions of continuing inequality and oppression, this would merely 'entrench the rights of right holders and the rightlessness of the rightless'.[180]

Sachs and Asmal, both rebellious spirits with a persuasive ability to reach out to international as well as domestic constitutional experts, took a lead in publicising the virtues of human rights by naturalising it within a long resistance tradition. Writing in 1992, Asmal insisted that the 'oppressed do not have to *develop* a culture of human rights as a rich vein exists in the fabric of the liberation movement'. And he went on to co-author a book to prove the point.[181] Sachs also produced a book in which he announced: '[we are] discovering the full potential for our country of the application of universally held concepts of human rights. We are finding that principles which might be conservative in other countries are transformatory, even revolutionary in ours.' Here he spoke with the seductive moral and political passion of the convert: Sachs admitted that his own ideas had developed markedly since the 1950s when he was 'a new revolutionary, idealistic about people, sceptical about the law'. Now, he acknowledged, 'we are realizing that constitutionalism, far from being a brake on democracy, offers the best chance of realizing the ideals set out in the Freedom Charter.'[182]

Setting the new nation to rights

Among the many parallels between the history of Afrikaner and African nationalism is their near simultaneous – and, frankly, unlikely – rediscovery of the utility of human rights from the mid-1980s.[183] This occurred at the height of the ongoing state of emergency, which tipped the country close to anarchy and civil war. The Codesa and Multi-Party Negotiating Process took place at the same time as the government and the ANC were effectively at war; both adversaries were pursuing a dangerous dual strategy which combined destabilisation and armed struggle, on the one hand, with rapprochement, on the other. The fall of the Berlin Wall and the disintegration of the Soviet Union changed the political landscape by removing key support for the ANC as well as the communist bogy upon which apartheid propaganda depended so heavily. Operating from different premises and with different ends in mind, key politicians on both sides came to accept that new ways had to be found to break the dangerous deadlock. In both cases, there was an overlap between those who favoured rights and those who were disposed towards negotiations; this set them apart from those on either side who felt that the conflict should be settled militarily.

Secret negotiations between the government and the ANC began around 1987, often brokered by liberal- or social democratic-minded intermediaries in Europe. It was around this time that opinion-formers in the government and the ANC came to reassess the value of human rights discourse. The moment was propitious for the re-emergence, internationally and domestically, of liberal thought around rights and constitutionalism. Initially, tactical calculation rather than idealism dominated the thinking of the government and the ANC. But as the process developed there was a genuine sense of epiphany arising out of the realisation of a shared, historic breakthrough. In short, key leaders of the ANC gradually came round to the view, or were confirmed in their view, that the long-promised 'seizure of power' by armed means was unlikely. There was also widespread recognition of the real gains that had been made by democratic and 'civil society' forces within the country (led by the UDF), which were increasingly foregrounding 'rights'. Responsibilities of citizenship were also coming to the fore as the ANC contemplated the dangers of assuming administrative responsibility in a country that had nearly been rendered 'ungovernable'. For its part, voices within the government and state (including the judiciary) were beginning to accept that the security forces' destabilisation strategies were counterproductive, that official insistence on 'group' (ethnic) rights was unsustainable, and that legally entrenched individual rights might be the most efficacious means of defending existing economic privileges and future political freedoms. As the government shifted from consociationalism (ethnic power-sharing) to constitutionalism (the separation of legal powers), so the principle of the rule *of* law began to gain ground over the practice of rule *by* law or, in the context of the 1980s, extra-judicial fiat.

This new space encouraged interest in liberal constitutional principles which had long been marginalised in public discussion. International and South African-based experts on constitutional rights sought to mediate between two nationalisms, neither of which possessed the ability to defeat each other decisively, and both of which increasingly depended on each other's willingness to cooperate. The leading liberal power-broker, Frederik van Zyl Slabbert, who played a singular role in helping to break the political logjam from the mid-1980s, took the view that majority

115

rule backed by constitutionally entrenched individual rights was the best way forward. He wryly notes of the ANC and the government: 'through numerous engagements I had with both of them before 1990, they made it quite clear that a liberal democracy was the worst possible option for a future South Africa.'[184] A similar story is told by Johan van der Vyver, who conferred with the ANC in Harare in 1989 as part of a lawyers' conference brokered by Idasa.[185]

Hard calculation rather than unbridled idealism was evident on both sides – though it is also the case that the cathartic effect of throwing off the bonds of the past and participating in the miracle of the 'new' South Africa encouraged pragmatism to be restated as principle. As Heinz Klug explains, the new acceptance of rights thinking in terms of a 'globalising constitutionalism' became 'both a natural way for élites to think and a passport to international acceptability'.[186] By 1993, all parties who were serious about political negotiations in South Africa were committed to some version of a constitutionally entrenched bill of rights. It is therefore highly significant that discussions about rights played a leading role as an ideological solvent in the lead-up to formal negotiations between government and opposition, and more so in the complex bargaining that took place between 1991 and 1994; that is, rights were not merely tacked on as an appendage in the process of tying up loose legal ends. This was a distinctive aspect of South Africa's political transition, as remarkable in its own way as the Truth and Reconciliation Commission, which has attracted rather more expert attention.

Doreen Atkinson's account of the proceedings of the 'technical committee' which worked on the bill of rights as part of the 1993 Multi-Party Negotiation Process confirms that the intensive process of bargaining and compromise itself played a notable role in brokering the transition to a new political order.[187] Yet, the fact that the bargaining was conducted behind closed doors meant that public scrutiny and approval were deferred. This may have had negative consequences for the long-run legitimacy of the process, especially for critics within the ANC government who today maintain that deals were done which have compromised the national democratic revolution. In 2011 the senior ANC member Ngoako Ramatlhodi declared that the Constitution 'reflects the great compromise, a compromise tilted heavily in favour of forces against change'. The ANC Youth League populist Julius Malema followed up with a claim that the 'untransformed' judiciary is a vehicle for reintroducing apartheid through the 'back door'.[188] Such perceptions easily feed into a much longer view that law has always operated on a racial basis. As the legal historian Martin Chanock predicted a decade ago: 'people with all their eggs in the new rights-based formalist basket will be disappointed. Neither law nor rights will trump politics, particularly as both may depend on an administrative capacity that the state may not have.'[189]

An advanced Bill of Rights professing itself the 'cornerstone of democracy in South Africa' lies at the heart of the final Constitution which came into force in 1997 – an outcome that could hardly have been seriously anticipated at the start of the decade. By endorsing the principle of constitutional supremacy as a founding value, the country ended an unbroken tradition of parliamentary sovereignty dating back to 1910. More fundamentally still, its founding values herald a distinct break from a past based on racial oppression and exploitation. In this sense, the Constitution is at once a memorial to the past and also a monument which builds upon the foundations of the country's transition to democracy in order to look to the future.[190]

The first chapter of the Constitution specifies 'Human dignity, the achievement of equality and the advancement of human rights and freedoms' as fundamental values (along with non-racism, non-sexism, the rule of law and universal adult suffrage). Chapter 2 comprises a justiciable Bill of Rights, widely considered by jurists to be one of the most progressive in the world: in addition to fundamental first-order rights, it entrenches substantial second-generation socio-economic rights (the 'right to expect') such as access to food, water, housing, health care, education and social security, as well as the special rights of children. It is the first constitution in the world to prohibit discrimination on the grounds of sexual orientation. A number of standing commissions were also created, including those dedicated to Gender Equality, Land Rights and Human Rights. In 2007 a multi-party committee set up by parliament to review the functioning of these 'Chapter 9' institutions was established after concerns that they were proving less efficacious than intended. Little has come of the committee's recommendations, other than the creation of a parliamentary Office on Institutions Supporting Democracy whose status and functions, in 2011, remain opaque.[191]

Public awareness of human rights has been maintained to an extent by the celebration of a public holiday on 21 March (the anniversary of the 1960 Sharpeville massacre) as Human Rights Day. More importantly, public engagement was promoted by the Truth and Reconciliation Commission, set up in 1995.[192] Its Human Rights Violation Committee investigated 'gross' human rights abuses (such as killings, abductions, torture and severe ill-treatment) that occurred between 1960 and 1994, and took evidence in public from witnesses across the country. In this manner human rights became central to the process of restorative justice and human dignity which the TRC was committed to uphold as part of its efforts to 'heal' the body politic of a damaged society. The public recounting of experiences of suffering and pain has been widely criticised as an inadequate substitute for effective legal and material restitution. A counter-view is that emotions are key to the mobilisation of a human rights consciousness and are 'essential to the reconstitution of the self and the remaking of a social world'.[193]

For many analysts the Truth and Reconciliation Commission was a defining process in the transition to post-apartheid nationhood. Yet, despite the massive publicity that attended its proceedings, the Truth and Reconciliation Commission has faded from recent collective memory. So, too, has its underlying philosophy of *ubuntu*, which, in defining the essence of 'being human' in terms of one's interconnectedness with others, mixed together human rights, restorative justice, reconciliation and nation-building within an inclusive sense of communal Africanism.[194] Thabo Mbeki provided a lead when, as President, he gave the TRC's final report only cursory acknowledgement and proceeded to supplant the watchword of *ubuntu* with the more assertive claims of the 'African Renaissance'. The government has proved dilatory and parsimonious in paying reparations to victims, itself an indication of official detachment from the national reconciliation agenda.[195] Today, the thrust of public moral outrage is focused more on issues like corruption, crime and ongoing social inequality.

Although not so well publicised as the TRC, and certainly not so extensively written about by academics outside the legal profession, the discussions about constitutional rights in the period leading up to the first democratic elections were vital to the success of the transition and lent legal substance to the transition in ways that the TRC was unable to achieve. Debates around the government's commitment to the constitutionally entrenched rights remain a live political concern. The statutory Human Rights Commission has been largely ineffectual and reactive.[196] In its conduct of foreign affairs, which for a brief moment after 1994 was shaped by explicit commitments to a human rights agenda, the Mbeki presidency's embrace of anti-imperialism and 'Africanism' has led South Africa to provide diplomatic protection to the likes of Mugabe in Zimbabwe and Bashir in the Sudan.[197] President Zuma's inconsistent approach to the crisis in Libya in 2011, and to Gaddafi in particular, raises further questions about the country's willingness to adhere to its human rights agenda. The government's refusal to permit the entry of the Dalai Lama into South Africa in 2011, widely seen as a concession to China, was another low point.

The Constitutional Court has delivered several landmark judgments which have attracted positive comments by legal experts abroad and in South Africa.[198] The outlawing of capital punishment in 1995 by reference to the constitutional right to life (and the values of *ubuntu*) was an auspicious start. Yet, in a country racked by violence and vulnerable to vengeance, this judgment did not command widespread popular support. Notably, the new policing services have struggled to reconcile their role as law enforcers with the new human rights culture they were enjoined to embrace. In 2000 Mbeki's no-nonsense Minister of Safety and Security, Steve Tshwete, gave voice to the widespread desire for tough policing, even including lethal force, in the following terms: 'Criminals must know that the South African Police possesses the authority, moral and political, to ensure by all means, constitutional or unconstitutional, that the people of this country are not deprived of their human rights.'[199]

In a society that remains deeply divided and traumatised by its past the Constitutional Court's legitimacy is subject to political contestation. It is too early to know whether the Court will be able to defend the independence of the judiciary or, indeed, itself from attack by leading politicians. In 2008 the ANC secretary-general Gwede Mantashe was quoted as accusing the judiciary and the Constitutional Court of having a 'counter-revolutionary agenda' – a reference to the highly politicised controversy over Cape judge president John Hlophe and its alleged campaign against President Zuma.[200] But if senior politicians fail to defend the Court – or attempt to control it through manipulation and patronage (as Zuma's 2011 nomination of Mogoeng Mogoeng as 'preferred candidate' for Chief Justice suggests)[201] – its authority stands to be undermined. A key test will be how (and if) the Constitutional Court deals with the Protection of Information (Secrecy) Bill, which many regard as an attempt by the state to muzzle press freedom.[202]

The independence of the Constitutional Court may also be at risk if proposals to make it the 'apex court' (a supreme court) compromise its capacity to rule on strictly constitutional matters, including the second-order socio-economic rights which are entrenched in the Bill of Rights. Key judgments such as the *Government of the Republic of South Africa and Others* v. *Grootboom and Others* (2000), dealing with the right to housing and shelter, have brought the Constitutional Court into conflict with the government. So, too, did the Court's decision in *Minister of Health and Others* v. *Treatment Action Campaign and Others* (2002), which found that the government had acted unreasonably and contrary to the Bill of Rights in refusing to allow anti-retroviral drugs to be administered on a large scale to HIV-positive mothers of infants.

The Court's responsibility to defend personal freedoms conflicts with broader social attitudes. Its judgment outlawing the death penalty was, and most likely remains, at variance with the instincts of the populace and the police, who face extreme levels of violence on a constant basis. In the view of the law professor Lourens du Plessis, the Court's decision, arising out of its interpretation of the Constitution's 'right to life' provision, exposed underlying rifts on the issue of capital punishment, with negative consequences for the Court's credibility and the administration of justice.[203] Similarly, a considerable gulf exists between popular attitudes towards gender and homosexuality – 'corrective' rapes of lesbians are not uncommonly perpetrated – and the progressive provisions of the Constitution. There is also wide disparity between the Constitution's explicit recognition of the rights of non-citizens (in line with the sentiment of the Freedom Charter) and popular attitudes to African immigrants (legal and non-legal) and refugees, who have been subject to regular campaigns of violence (commonly referred to as 'xenophobia').[204] Here the tension between citizenship (for South African-born blacks) and human rights (for African people more generally) emerges with brutal clarity.

When the Constitution was finalised in 1996 it was often remarked that a shared *culture* of human rights had yet to embed itself in South African society.[205] Whether this is now happening remains uncertain. Should this occur, it is likely to take shape in campaigns 'from below' led by activists concerned to advance the rights of those suffering from HIV/Aids, or seeking land redistribution, tenure for urban squatters, better provision of health and education, and protection of migrants.[206] The role of the trade unions, a powerful constituency with a strong tradition of independent thinking, is also important. So, too, are the universities and the media. One thing seems certain: the moment of constitution-making 'from above', which helped to secure the political process of transition to the post-apartheid era, is over.

Notes

Chapter 1: Introduction

1 Hugh Corder, 'Constitution Reigns Whether Zuma Likes It or Not', *Business Day*, 31.8.2011.

2 Arthur Chaskalson, 'The Fragility of Rights', in P.J. Salazar (ed.), *Under the Baobab: Essays to Honour Stuart Saunders on his Eightieth Birthday* (Cape Town, 2011), 10; Njabulo S. Ndebele, 'Renewing Citizenship', www.zapiro.com.

3 My thanks to Mark Mazower for help with this formulation.

4 I am not seeking here to make rigorous formal distinctions between these different kinds of rights, as, for example, helpfully essayed by the political philosopher Raymond Geuss in *History and Illusion in Politics* (Cambridge, 2001).

5 Kader Asmal with David Chidester and Cassius Lubisi, *Legacy of Freedom: The ANC's Human Rights Tradition* (Johannesburg, 2005). See also K. Asmal, *Politics in My Blood* (Johannesburg, 2011), 100, 105–6; 'Democracy and Human Rights: Developing a South African Human Rights Culture', *New England Law Journal* 27 (Winter 1992), 292; K. Asmal, L. Asmal and R.S. Roberts, *Reconciliation Through Truth*, 2nd edn (Cape Town, 1997), ch. 10.

6 B. Ackerman, 'The Rise of World Constitutionalism', *Occasional Papers*, Paper 4 (1996); http://digitalcommons.law.yale.edu.

7 S. Moyn, *The Last Utopia: Human Rights in History* (Cambridge, Mass., 2010), 3, 173.

8 Robin Blackburn, 'Reclaiming Human Rights', *New Left Review* 69 (May/June 2011), 135.

9 E. Borgwardt, *A New Deal for the World: America's Vision for*

Human Rights (Cambridge, Mass., 2007), 34, 29.

10 Karel Vasak, 'A 30-Year Struggle. The Sustained Efforts to Give Force of Law to the Universal Declaration of Human Rights', *Unesco Courier* (November 1977), 29. My thanks to Rob Skinner for alerting me to this article.

Chapter 2: Burgher republicanism and colonialism

11 At the end of the 18th century there were around 15,000 free burghers at the Cape.

12 G. Groenewald, 'An Early Modern Entrepreneur: Hendrik Oostwald Eksteen and the Creation of Wealth in Dutch Colonial Cape Town, 1702–1741', *Kronos* 35 (2009); T. Baartman, 'Protest and Dutch Burgher Identity', in N. Worden (ed.), *Cape Town Between East and West* (Johannesburg, 2012).

13 G. Schutte, 'Company and Colonists at the Cape, 1652–1795', in R. Elphick and H. Giliomee (eds.), *The Shaping of South African Society, 1652–1840* (Cape Town, 1989), 287. Schutte notes that 'The proposal in 1786 that the confusing term "civil rights" (*burgerregten*) be deleted from the letters conferring freeburgher status was fully in accord with Company views'. See also the illuminating discussion by Yvonne Brink, 'Changing Perceptions of Free Burgher Status and Identity at the Cape during the Period of VOC Rule', in N. Worden (ed.), *Contingent Lives: Social Identity and Material Culture in the VOC World* (Cape Town, 2007), 414–15.

14 For a recent extended discussion of the Cape's burgher gentry, see W. Dooling, *Slavery, Emancipation and Colonial Rule in South Africa* (Pietermaritzburg, 2007), ch. 1. Whereas landdrosts were salaried officials of the VOC, heemraden were unsalaried and drawn from the ranks of burghers.

15 H. Giliomee, '"Allowed Such a State of Freedom": Women and Gender Relations in the Afrikaner Community before Enfranchisement in 1930', *New Contree* 59 (2010).

16 The best discussion remains Nigel Penn, *Rogues, Rebels and Runaways: Eighteenth-Century Cape Characters* (Cape Town, 1999), ch. 3.

17 Schutte, 'Company and Colonists', 316.

18 Giliomee, *The Afrikaners: Biography of a People* (London,

2003), 74; see also A. du Toit and H. Giliomee, *Afrikaner Political Thought Analysis and Documents, vol. 1* (Berkeley and Cape Town, 1983).

19 Lyn Hunt, *Inventing Human Rights: A History* (New York, 2007), 135.

20 S. Huigen, *Knowledge and Colonialism: Eighteenth-Century Travellers in South Africa* (Leiden, 2009), 171–2.

21 John Barrow, *Travels into the Interior of Southern Africa in the Years 1797 and 1798, vol. 1* (London, 1801), 151–2, 157, 205–6.

22 C.A. Bayly, *Imperial Meridian: The British Empire and the World 1780–1830* (London, 1989), 202.

23 See Susan Maslan, 'The Anti-Human: Man and Citizen before the Declaration of the Rights of Man and of the Citizen', *South Atlantic Quarterly* 103, 2/3 (2004); also Moyn, *The Last Utopia*, 25–6.

Chapter 3: Humanitarianism

24 Giliomee, *The Afrikaners*, 105–7. Notwithstanding the fact that Stockenström – who regarded himself as an Afrikaner – was a slave-holder.

25 W.M. Macmillan, *The Cape Colour Question: A Historical Survey* (London, 1927), 212–13, 211n1; Albie Sachs, *Justice in South Africa* (Sussex, 1973), 18–19; T. Keegan, *Colonial South Africa and the Origins of the Racial Order* (Cape Town, 1996), 104. Ordinance 50 overturned the Caledon or 'Hottentot Code' of 1809, which had been introduced by the British to regularise the employment of indigenous peoples. Although purporting to give servants some protection by making contracts compulsory, the consensus of modern historians is that the real effect was to enforce conditions of servitude by, for instance, instituting rigorous pass controls.

26 Keegan, *Colonial South Africa*, 92; E. Elbourne, *Blood Ground: Colonialism, Missions and the Contest for Christianity in the Cape Colony and Britain, 1799–1853* (Montreal, 2002), 246ff.

27 Elbourne, *Blood Ground*, 256.

28 Cited in A. Lester, *Imperial Networks: Creating Identities in Nineteenth-Century South Africa and Britain* (London, 2001), 32.

29 A. Pagden, 'Human Rights, Natural Rights and Europe's Imperial Legacy', *Political Theory* 31, 2 (2003), 178.

30 R.A. Wilson and R.D. Brown (eds.), 'Introduction', in *Humanitarianism and Suffering: The Mobilization of Empathy* (Cambridge, 2009).

31 Hunt, *Inventing Human Rights*, 20–1, 26–7, 32.

32 D. Gorman, *Imperial Citizenship: Empire and the Question of Belonging* (Manchester, 2006), 9, 156.

33 F. Cooper and A.L. Stoler (eds.), *Tensions of Empire* (Berkeley, 1997), 2.

34 I owe this point to Alan Lester, who adds that Ordinance 50 might best be seen as a measure that altered the legal status of Khoekhoen by including them as subjects of the Crown and therefore not as aliens with whom a state of war could exist.

35 Under the British, the Cape also became the site of one of several Vice-Admiralty courts which exercised jurisdiction over naval matters and, after 1807, helped to suppress the slave trade in association with the courts of Mixed Commission (est. 1817). These courts, operating in a large arc from the coasts of West to East Africa (as well as the Caribbean and Latin America), assumed widespread powers to adjudicate when ships alleged to be engaged in the slave trade were captured. Anti-slaving patrols and the associated legal machinery helped Britain to consolidate its maritime influence and trading activities along the African littoral – and so suggest an early example of human rights providing the backing for foreign intervention. I owe this observation to Patrick Harries. For a useful general summary, see Leslie Bethell, 'The Mixed Commissions for the Suppression of the Transatlantic Slave Trade in the Nineteenth Century', *Journal of African History* 7, 1 (1966).

36 M. Chapman, *Southern African Literatures* (London, 1996), 98.

37 Giliomee, *The Afrikaners*, 113–14.

Chapter 4: Liberalism and its challenges

38 I have argued this at length in *A Commonwealth of Knowledge: Science, Sensibility and White South Africa 1820–2000* (Oxford, 2006).

39 Cited in A.F. Hattersley, *The Convict Crisis and the Growth*

of Unity: Resistance to Transportation in South Africa and Australia 1848–1853 (Pietermaritzburg, 1965), 80.

40 A. du Toit, 'The Cape Afrikaners' Failed Liberal Moment', in J. Butler, R. Elphick and D. Welsh (eds.), *Democratic Liberalism in South Africa: Its History and Prospect* (Middletown and Cape Town, 1987), 42.

41 Ibid., 44.

42 G. Le Sueur, *Cecil Rhodes: The Man and His Work* (London, 1914), 76. Rhodes originally specified 'white' men but corrected this after being challenged on the eve of a general election, when the 'non-white' vote was still a significant factor.

43 Cited in R. Parry, '"In a Sense Citizens, but Not Altogether Citizens …": Rhodes, Race, and the Ideology of Segregation at the Cape in the Late Nineteenth Century', *Canadian Journal of African Studies* 17, 3 (1983), 386.

44 H. Klug, *Constituting Democracy: Law, Globalism and South Africa's Political Reconstruction* (Cambridge, 2000), 33.

45 J. Bryce, *Impressions of South Africa*, 3rd edn (London, 1899), 314; M.C.E. van Schoor, 'The Orange Free State', in C.F.J. Muller (ed.), *500 Years: A History of South Africa*, 2nd edn (Pretoria, 1977), 234.

46 South African Law Commission, *Working Paper 25, Project 58: Group and Human Rights* (Pretoria, 1989), 214–15.

47 L.M. Thompson, 'Constitutionalism in the South African Republics', *Butterworth's South African Law Review* (1954), 55, 57ff.

48 On racially exclusive republicanism and the constitution of the Orange Free State, see H.J. van Aswegen, *Die Verhouding tussen Blank and Nie-Blank in die Oranje-Vrystaat, 1854–1902* (Pretoria, 1977), ch. 8.

49 J. Hyslop, 'The Imperial Working Class Makes Itself "White": White Labourism in Britain, Australia and South Africa before the First World War', *Journal of Historical Sociology* 12, 4 (1999).

50 F.W. Reitz, *A Century of Wrong* (London, [1900]), 3. Although issued by Reitz, it is generally accepted that J.C. Smuts had a major role in its authorship.

51 L.M. Thompson, *The Unification of South Africa* (Oxford, 1960), 97–101.

52 J. Dugard, 'Changing Attitudes towards a Bill of Rights in South Africa', in J.H. van der Westhuizen and H.P. Viljoen (eds.), *A Bill of Rights for South Africa* (Durban, 1988), 29. M.M. Corbett, 'Human Rights: The Road Ahead', in C.F. Forsyth and J.E. Schiller (eds.), *Human Rights: The Cape Town Conference* (Cape Town, 1979), 5.

53 SAPA, 1.11.2011, http://www.timeslive.co.za. For analysis, see Geoff Budlender's 2011 Bram Fischer Memorial Lecture, 11.11.2011; http://constitutionallyspeaking.co.za.

Chapter 5: Segregationism

54 This was the clear message of the *Report of the South African Native Affairs Commission 1903–1905* (Cd. 2399, 1905) whose terms of reference explicitly stated the need for comprehensive agreement on 'affairs relating to the Natives and Native administration' in the light of 'the coming Federation of South African Colonies'.

55 The free-thinking, radical woman of letters Olive Schreiner was distraught at the passage of the Natives Land Act of 1913, and invoked the idea of universal 'human rights' in doing so when she wrote to the liberal Cape politician John X. Merriman: 'If only we could awake South Africa to-day that though for the moment we can refuse the vote the right to hold land & nearly all other human rights to the vast native population of South Africa the day *is* coming, in less than 15 years when the millions will rise up & demand, what we might by generously giving them now win their love & gratitude.' (UCT Manuscripts, Olive Schreiner Papers, BC16, Box 3, Folder 4, 1905/38, O. Schreiner to Betty Molteno, 15.9.1905).

56 Gorman, *Imperial Citizenship*, 162.

57 I owe this point to Karin Harris.

58 J. Martens, 'A Transnational History of Immigration Restriction: Natal and New South Wales, 1896–97', *Journal of Imperial and Commonwealth History* 34, 3 (2006). The Natal Act was itself influenced by American and Australian legislation, indicating the rapid global circulation of legal

precedents and forms.

59 M. Mazower, *No Enchanted Palace: The End of Empire and the Ideological Origins of the United Nations* (Princeton, 2009).

60 J. Klaaren, 'Migrating to Citizenship: Mobility, Law, and Nationality in South Africa, 1897–1937' (Ph.D. thesis, Yale University, 2004).

61 M. Shain, *Jewry and Cape Society* (Cape Town, 1983), 130ff.

62 Cited in Asmal, *Legacy of Freedom*, 47.

63 R.V. Selope Thema, 'The Race Problem' (1922), doc. 52 in S.W. Johns and G. Gerhart, *From Protest to Challenge, vol. 1*, revised edn (Johannesburg, forthcoming).

64 S. Dubow, *Racial Segregation and the Origins of Apartheid in South Africa, 1919–36* (London, 1989), 163–4.

65 P. Limb, *The ANC's Early Years: Nation, Class and Place in South Africa before 1940* (Pretoria, 2009), 249.

Chapter 6: The Second World War and its aftermath

66 M. Lake and H. Reynolds, *Drawing the Global Colour Line* (Cambridge, 2008), 11–12, 337ff. The authors lay particular emphasis on the transforming effect of the Japanese military successes during the Second World War. For an excellent discussion of the concept of rights and citizenship in francophone Africa, see F. Cooper, 'Citizenship and the Politics of Difference in French Africa, 1946–1960', in H. Fischer-Tiné and S. Ghermann, *Empires and Boundaries* (New York, 2009).

67 T. Karis and G. Gerhart (eds.), *From Protest to Challenge, vol. 2*, rev. edn (Johannesburg, forthcoming), doc. 32. See also SADET, *The Road to Democracy: South Africans Telling Their Stories, vol. 1* (Johannesburg, 2008), ch. 1, testimony of Joe Matthews, 9, 16.

68 Borgwardt, *A New Deal for the World*, 28, 29. Borgwardt oversimplifies for effect when she suggests that it was Mandela himself who inspired the ANC's interpretation of the Atlantic Charter. The committee responsible for drafting *Africans' Claims* was chaired by Z.K. Matthews. Mandela was not directly involved.

69 Luli Callinicos, *Oliver Tambo: Beyond the Engeli Mountains* (Cape Town, 2004), 145.

70 Asmal, *Legacy of Freedom*, 5. The sentence that follows is more convincing: 'Here is an indigenous African document, far ahead of developments in the rest of the world, which worked out basic human rights in the face of their denial.'

71 S. Dubow and A. Jeeves (eds.), *South Africa's 1940s: Worlds of Possibilities* (Cape Town, 2005).

72 M. Sherwood, '"There Is No New Deal for the Blackman in San Francisco": African Attempts to Influence the Founding Conference of the United Nations, April–July 1945', *International Journal of African Historical Studies* 29, 1 (1996), 72–3, 81; U. Oji Umozurike, *The African Charter on Human and Peoples' Rights* (The Hague, 1997), 24. In India, Gandhi was quick to point out that the Atlantic Charter's statements on democracy rang hollow in colonial Asia and Africa.

73 Enuga S. Reddy, a young Indian intern at the United Nations in 1948, grew interested in South Africa partly through meeting Alphaeus Hunton of the Council on African Affairs. Over the course of a long career at the United Nations, during which he served as secretary of the Special Committee Against Apartheid and director of its Center Against Apartheid, Reddy became an expert international interlocutor for the anti-apartheid movement and an ongoing Gandhian link between India, the UN and South Africa.

74 R. Skinner, *The Foundations of Anti-Apartheid* (Basingstoke, 2010), 69ff. I am grateful to Rob Skinner for supplying me with a copy of the Campaign for Right and Justice manifesto, located in Wits Historical Papers, SAIRR AD843/RJ/PC1.

75 Mazower, *No Enchanted Palace*, 7–8.

76 Thompson, *Unification of South Africa*, 119.

77 S. Dubow, 'Smuts, the United Nations and the Rhetoric of Race and Rights', *Journal of Contemporary History* 43, 1 (2008), 43–72.

78 Gorman, *Imperial Citizenship*, 15.

79 J. Seekings, 'Visions, Hopes and Views about the Future: The Radical Moment of South African Welfare Reform', in Dubow and Jeeves, *South Africa's 1940s*, 50.

80 M. Wilson, *Freedom for My People: The Autobiography of Z.K. Matthews: Southern Africa 1901–1968* (Cape Town, 1981), 149ff.

81 M. Swan, 'Ideology in Organised Indian Politics, 1891–1948', in S. Marks and S. Trapido (eds.), *Politics of Race, Class and Nationalism* (London, 1987), 203; also C. Sarma, 'Smuts, Satyagraha, and Human Rights: The 1946–1948 South African Indian Passive Resistance Campaign' (M.Sc. African Studies dissertation, Oxford University, 2011).

82 www.sacp.org.za.

Chapter 7: Anti-apartheid

83 www.sacp.org.za.

84 Letter from W.M. Sisulu to Prime Minister D.F. Malan on behalf of the African National Congress, 21.1.1952 and reply from M. Aucamp, 29.1.1952; www.anc.org.za.

85 D. Everatt, 'Alliance Politics of a Special Type: The Roots of the ANC/SACP Alliance, 1950–1954', *Journal of Southern African Studies* 18, 1 (1991).

86 The 1954 Women's Charter claimed, 'Equal rights with men in relation to property, marriage and children, and for the removal of all laws and customs that deny women such equal rights'; http://sadtu-pol-ed.blogspot.com. See the analysis offered by Cherryl Walker, *Women and Resistance in South Africa* (London, 1982), 156–8; and Ray Alexander Simons, *All My Life and All My Strength* (Johannesburg, 2004), 269–70.

87 The Liberal Party's objections are detailed by Randolph Vigne in *Liberals against Apartheid* (London, 1997), ch. 6.

88 Wilson, *Freedom for My People*, 171, 173. The demand for a 'national convention' recalled the All-African Convention of the 1930s and may have evoked the pre-Union convention of 1908–9 in some minds. Demands for a national convention were made by many organisations in the 1950s and early 1960s.

89 Wits Historical Papers, Ba3.6, Annexure A1, 'Memorandum on the Congress of the People Submitted by ANC to the Conference of Sponsoring Organisations on 21 March 1954'.

90 Rusty Bernstein, *Memory against Forgetting* (London, 1999), 145, 142–3.

91 Conspiracy theories notwithstanding, the evidence presented by Joshua Lazerson tracing the affinities between

'Marxist lectures' produced by the Congress of Democrats and circulated prior to the Congress of the People makes for interesting reading, particularly in the light of Rusty Bernstein's major role in drafting the Charter. Lazerson shows that the lecture 'Change Is Needed' criticised parliament as a key ruling-class instrument and instead favoured a 'People's Democracy' (J. Lazerson, *Against the Tide: Whites in the Struggle against Apartheid* (Boulder and Cape Town, 1994), 121–3).

92 UCT Manuscripts, Z.K. Matthews Papers (microfilm), BCZA B2.32, 'Supplement to Existing Statement', 1–2.

93 T. Karis and G. Gerhart (eds.), *From Protest to Challenge, vol. 3: Challenge and Violence, 1953–1964* (Johannesburg, 2012), 57.

94 Lazerson, *Against the Tide*, 177.

95 Ibid., ch. 8.

96 See for example D.M. Davis, 'The Rule of Law and the Radical Debate', *Acta Juridica* (Cape Town, 1981), 65–82.

Chapter 8: Internationalising rights

97 Lorna Lloyd, '"A Family Quarrel": Development of the Dispute over Indians in South Africa', *Historical Journal* 34, 3 (1991), 724.

98 R.B. Ballinger, 'UN Action on Human Rights in South Africa', in E. Luard (ed.), *The International Protection of Human Rights* (London, 1967), 248, 254.

99 Schifter points out that, whereas other violators were members of voting blocs of substantial size at the UN, South Africa was isolated. Thus, 'it very well may have required a friendless, racist human rights violator such as South Africa to break down the barriers that stood in the way of United Nations scrutiny of a member state's abusive treatment of its own citizens.' It took more than 20 years before another friendless country, Chile, was subjected to specific criticism for its domestic violations of human rights. See R. Schifter, 'Human Rights at the United Nations: The South Africa Precedent', *American University Journal of International Law and Policy* 8 (1993), 362–3, 370.

100 *Report of the United Nations Commission on the Racial Situation in the Union of South Africa*, A/2505 and Add.1, 1953.

See Schifter, 'Human Rights at the United Nations', 365, 366.

101 Ballinger, 'UN Action', 254, 258.

102 For example, the independent-minded Nationalist politician and diplomat R.F. ('Pik') Botha advised the government in 1970 to adopt the UN Declaration of Human Rights; four years later, as Minister of Foreign Affairs, he disingenuously informed the United Nations that he could not defend apartheid.

103 G. Houser, 'Meeting Africa's Challenge: The Story of the American Committee on Africa' (1976), www.aluka.org.

104 For example, letter from Albert Luthuli to ACOA, 6.8.1962 (co-sponsored by Martin Luther King, Jr.), and appeal by Glenn Moss, Human Rights Committee, Johannesburg, to ACOA, 3.12.1974, www.aluka.org.

105 Carol Anderson, *Eyes off the Prize: The United Nations and the African American Struggle for Human Rights, 1944–1955* (New York, 2003), chs. 3 and 4; Skinner, *The Foundations of Anti-Apartheid*, 149–50.

106 *The Times*, 10.12.1957, 11.12.1957. The Dean of Cape Town, the Rev. J. Savage, told a crowd of 400 assembled outside St George's Cathedral that 'The right of full citizenship should not depend on race but on fitness to discharge that right'.

107 R. Skinner, 'The Moral Foundations of British Anti-Apartheid Activism, 1946–1960', *Journal of Southern African Studies* 35, 2 (2009).

108 'Statement on Human Rights Year by Oliver Tambo', 1.6.1968, www.anc.org.za.

109 H. Thörn, *Anti-Apartheid and the Emergence of a Global Civil Society* (Basingstoke, 2006), 68–9, 79.

110 J. Dugard, *Human Rights and the South African Legal Order* (New Jersey, 1987), 46–9; J. Dugard, 'Human Rights and the Rule of Law, I', in Butler, Elphick and Welsh, *Democratic Liberalism in South Africa*, 273–4.

111 W.W.M. Eiselen, 'Harmonious Multi-Community Development', *Optima* 9, 1 (1959), 3–5.

112 'American Ways "More Threat to S.A. than the Reds"', *Pretoria News*, 19.10.1966, NAACP Records, Part VI: 1961–1972, Box VI: A15, Africa, South Africa, 1966–1967. I am grateful to Zoe

Hyman for this reference.

113 On the significance of President Carter's invocation of human rights more generally, see Moyn, *The Last Utopia*, 149ff.

114 C. Coker, 'Retreat into the Future: The United States, South Africa, and Human Rights, 1976–8', *Journal of Modern African Studies* 18, 3 (1980), 521–2. This line of argument can be traced back at least as far as Verwoerd's impromptu response to Macmillan's 1960 'Wind of Change' address, in which the South African premier insisted that whites in Africa were also deserving of 'justice'.

115 The League, which was inaugurated to campaign against the threat to the Coloured vote, acted to campaign in favour of civil rights as well as providing a broad educative role.

116 M. Legassick and C. Saunders, 'Aboveground Activity in the 1960s', in SADET, *The Road to Democracy in South Africa, vol. 1 (1960–1970)* (Cape Town, 2004), 679.

117 Vigne, *Liberals against Apartheid*, 77; Lazerson, *Against the Tide*, 199–200.

118 UCT Manuscripts, Z.K. Matthews Papers (microfilm), BCZA B3.51, B3.54, letters to Matthews from Dennis Brutus, D. van der Ross, J.C.A. Daniels; also B3.61, 'Towards a National Convention' by D. Brutus.

119 Dugard, 'Changing Attitudes towards a Bill of Rights in South Africa', 30–1. In 1988 the League reached out of its natural constituency when it organised a forum discussion on *A South African Bill of Rights* (Cape Town, 1989) in association with the University of the Western Cape Law Centre. In his preface to the proceedings, the president of the League, former principal of the University of Cape Town, Richard Luyt, only slightly exaggerated when he said that the subject was one 'which the direct experience of South Africans is virtually and sadly NIL!' The political philosopher André du Toit provided much-needed conceptual clarification in his contribution 'What Rights Should Be Included as Human and Civil Rights in South Africa', as well as in discussion. See also Du Toit's address to the Civil Rights League on *The Politics of Civil Rights* (Cape Town, 1977).

120 J.J. Human, *South Africa 1960* (Cape Town, 1961), 199–202.

121 The Black Sash was originally founded by Jean Sinclair and five other women as the Women's League for the Defence of the Constitution. Sinclair's daughter Sheena Duncan (1932–2010) took over the Black Sash in 1975 and became known as one of South Africa's most effective human rights campaigners.

122 'Letter from the Black Sash', *Pro Veritate* 10, 5 (1971), 14, 7.

123 A. Sachs, *Protecting Human Rights in a New South Africa* (Cape Town, 1990), chs. 5–7.

124 Arthur Chaskalson became the first President of South Africa's post-apartheid Constitutional Court. On his work at the Legal Resources Centre, see Chaskalson's 1999 oral testimony at www.columbia.edu.

125 Charles Villa-Vicencio, *A Theology of Reconstruction: Nation-Building and Human Rights* (Cambridge, 1992).

126 *The Guardian*, 10.8.1978.

127 Ndungane's views are summarised in his article 'Human Rights', in C. Villa-Vicencio, and J.W. de Gruchy (eds.), *Doing Ethics in Context: South African Perspectives* (Maryknoll, NY, and Cape Town, 1994).

128 J.D. van der Vyver, *Menseregte* (Potchefstroom, 1974); *Seven Lectures on Human Rights* (Cape Town, 1976), 51–2, 120–1. See also the discussion of changing attitudes by Afrikaner theologians to human rights in South African Law Commission, *Project 58: Group and Human Rights* (Pretoria, 1989), 183ff.

129 Forsyth and Schiller, *Human Rights*.

130 *South African Journal of Human Rights* (editorial) 1, 1 (1985).

131 G.P.C. Kotzé, 'Menseregte: Suid-Afrika se Dilemma', in J.H. van der Westhuizen and H.P. Viljoen (eds.), *A Bill of Rights for South Africa* (Durban, 1988), 6.

Chapter 9: The embrace of human rights

132 Pippa Green, *Choice, Not Fate: The Biography of Trevor Manuel* (Johannesburg, 2008), 200.

133 Jeremy Seekings, *The UDF: A History of the United Democratic Front in South Africa 1983–1991* (Cape Town, 2000), 111.

134 Ibid., 119, instances the 1985 decision by UDF patrons to invite Edward Kennedy to South Africa as a moment where

tensions between the struggle for democratic or 'liberal rights' and the anti-capitalist demands of a liberation movement became evident.

135 T.D. Moodie, 'The Rise and Demise of Lira Setona? Questions of Race and How the NUM Became a Social Movement Union' (keynote address to Historical Association of South Africa conference, Potchefstroom, 2010).

136 See for example 'Fight for Your Rights', Chemical Workers' Industrial Union, March 1988', doc. 149 in G.M. Gerhart and C.L. Glaser, *From Protest to Challenge: A Documentary History of African Politics in South Africa 1882–1990, vol. 6* (Bloomington, Indiana, 2010), 644–6.

137 Albie Sachs Papers, Mayibuye Centre, UWC, MCH91, Box 9, 'Cosatu/ANC Workshop on Worker Rights and the New Constitution', 26.9.1991.

138 Kader Asmal, a long-term ANC and Communist Party member, had been a lecturer in law at Trinity College, Dublin. He was a founder member of the Irish Council for Civil Liberties. Albie Sachs was Professor of Law at the Eduardo Mondlane University in Maputo, Mozambique, and served as Director of Research in the Ministry of Justice. After nearly being killed by a car bomb in 1988, he returned to England where he became the founding Director of the South Africa Constitution Studies Centre at the Institute of Commonwealth Studies, University of London. He served as a judge in the post-apartheid Constitutional Court.

139 The text of the ANC's Constitutional Guidelines is reprinted in Sachs, *Protecting Human Rights*, Appendix 2.

140 Albie Sachs, interviewed by Gail Gerhart, Johannesburg, 29.11.1997, in Karis–Carter Collection, Wits Historical Papers, Cullen Library.

141 Asmal, *Politics in My Blood*, 107–9.

142 D. Chidester, 'Atlantic Community, Atlantic World: Anti-Americanism between Europe and Africa', *Journal of American History* 93, 2 (2006).

143 See for example *New York Times*, 11.12.1984; 15.1.1985; *Apdusa Bulletin 9*, 'The Kennedy Visit', www.aluka.org.

144 L. Bowman, 'South Africa's Southern Strategy and Its

Implications for the United States', *International Affairs* 47, 1 (1971), 27; C. Coker, 'The United States and South Africa: Can Constructive Engagement Succeed?', *Millennium* 11, 3 (1982), 225.

145 Ibid., 27.

146 See Simon Stevens's '"From the Viewpoint of a Southern Governor": The Carter Administration and Apartheid, 1977–81', *Diplomatic History* (forthcoming).

147 *The Guardian*, 6.9.1991; P. Trewelha, 'The Dilemma of Albie Sachs: ANC Constitutionalism and the Death of Thami Zulu', reprinted in *Inside Quatro: Uncovering the Exile History of the ANC and Swapo* (Johannesburg, 2009). For general context, see Amnesty International's report, *South Africa: Torture, Ill-treatment and Executions in African National Congress Camps*, 2.12.1992, www.amnesty.org. Documents in Sachs's personal collection at the Mayibuye Centre, MCH91, Box 8, reveal Sachs as a principled opponent of torture and violence, whatever the 'revolutionary' justification. My thanks to Olivia Greene for thoughts on the Code, which she sees as a significant development in the ANC's acceptance of constitutionalism and rights. Greene argues that acceptance of the Code was resisted by those in the ANC who continued to support a harsh disciplinary approach to alleged miscreants.

148 Cited in Seekings, *The UDF*, 242–3. Seekings notes that both the ANC in exile and Nelson Mandela felt that Morobe's press statement had 'gone too far'.

149 The commission chaired by Louis Skweyiya was 'left with an overall impression that for the better part of the 80's, there existed a situation of extraordinary abuse of power and lack of accountability. Nobody was beyond the reach of the security apparatus'; www.anc.org.za. See T. Lodge, 'Spectres from the Camps: The ANC's Commission of Enquiry', *Southern African Report* 8 (1993), 19–21. Cf. Asmal's account in *Politics in My Blood*, 168ff.

150 J.D. van der Vyver, 'Constitutional Options for Post-Apartheid South Africa', *Emory Law Journal* 40 (1991), 765n76. The TRC did not accept the view that human rights violations committed by the liberation movement in a 'just war' should

be treated differently in principle from abuses perpetrated by the state. The ANC's reaction to the TRC Report in 1999 was highly critical of the principle of 'even-handedness' in respect of gross human rights violations.

151 As Albie Sachs put it in 'Bill of Rights for South Africa: Areas of Agreement and Disagreement', *Columbia Human Rights Law Review* 21, 13 (1989–1990), 16, 'It is almost as if an inverse relationship exists between the adoption of a Bill of Rights and respect for human rights – the more grandiose the language of the Bill, the more likely it is that rights will be abused.'

152 Asmal, *Politics in My Blood*, 103.

153 Asmal, *Legacy of Freedom*, 73. A memorandum by the ANC's Constitution Committee to the ANC National Executive in September 1986 laid out basic constitutional guidelines; this included a Bill of Rights based on the Freedom Charter. See ANC Archives, Mayibuye Centre, UWC, MCH01-71.

154 www.constitutionnet.org.

155 P. Waldmeier, *Anatomy of a Miracle: The End of Apartheid and the Birth of the New South Africa* (Harmondsworth, 1998), 228.

156 These were Hugh Corder, Lourens du Plessis, Gerrit Grové and Zac Yacoob. Sbongile Nene was a sociologist. A notable omission was the Democratic Party's nominee, the human rights law expert John Dugard.

157 H. Corder, 'Prisoner, Partisan and Patriarch: Transforming the Law in South Africa 1985–2000', *South African Law Journal* 118, 4 (2001), 782–3.

158 H. Corder et al., *A Charter for Social Justice: A Contribution to the South African Bill of Rights Debate* (Cape Town, 1992).

159 Hugh Corder, 'South Africa's First Bill of Rights: Random Recollections of One of Its Drafters', *International Journal of Legal Information* 32, 2 (2004), 316–17; R. Spitz with M. Chaskalson, *The Politics of Transition: A Hidden History of South Africa's Negotiated Settlement* (Johannesburg, 2000), 50–1, 252ff; D.M. Davis, 'Constitutional Borrowing: The Influence of Legal Culture and Local History in the Reconstitution of Comparative Influence: The South African Experience', *International Journal of Constitutional Law* 1, 2 (2003), 185–9, 194.

160 Spitz and Chaskalson, *The Politics of Transition*, 265, 409 and 258ff.

161 L. du Plessis and H. Corder, *Understanding South Africa's Transitional Bill of Rights* (Cape Town, 1994), 40–1.

162 P. de Vos, 'A Bill of Rights in a Post-Apartheid South African Constitution: A Contextual International Human Rights Analysis', *Columbia Human Rights Law Review* 24, 277 (1992-3), 278.

163 Jennifer Clare Mohamed, 'Collective Rights, Transformation and Democracy', in G. Naidoo (ed.), *Reform and Revolution* (Johannesburg, 1991); Sachs, *Protecting Human Rights in a New South Africa*.

164 Cited in Doreen Atkinson, 'Insuring the Future? The Bill of Rights', in S. Friedman and D. Atkinson (eds.), *South African Review 7: The Small Miracle. South Africa's Negotiated Settlement* (Randburg, 1994), 123.

165 Dugard, 'Human Rights and the Rule of Law'.

166 J. Meierhenrich, *The Legacies of Law* (Cambridge, 2008), 295.

167 South African Law Commission, *Project 58: Group and Human Rights*; J. Dugard (editorial), 'A Bill of Rights for South Africa: Can the Leopard Change Its Spots?', *South African Journal for Human Rights* 2 (1986), 275, 276. Dugard points out that in 1984 Coetsee had himself pronounced against a bill of rights.

168 The South African Law Commission's *Project 58: Group and Human Rights* (1989) runs to nearly 500 pages and includes a lengthy consideration of the philosophy of human rights. One of its key conclusions (p. 41) states: 'Our survey of the main, currently relevant, schools of thought shows that the idea of the existence of certain fundamental human rights is a recurring theme in most philosophical movements. It is only in the extreme form of positivism, where moral considerations are placed outside the science of law, that there is no room for the existence of fundamental human rights.'

169 Van der Vyver, 'Constitutional Options', 757–8; *Group and Human Rights* (Pretoria, 1989). De Vos, 'A Bill of Rights in a Post-Apartheid South African Constitution', 286–7.

170 Hansard, 31.1.1986, cols. 13–14, cited in South African Law Commission, *Project 58: Group and Human Rights*, 265; 'Basic

Political Values for the Survival of the Afrikaner', 'strictly confidential' Afrikaner Broederbond document, c.1990, in ANC Archives, London Restricted Documents file, MCH02-57, Mayibuye Centre, UWC.

171 'Speech delivered by Gerrit Viljoen, Budget Debate: Constitutional Development: 11 May 1990', in Albie Sachs Papers, Mayibuye Centre, MCH91, Box 4b.

172 Asmal, *Politics in My Blood*, 114.

173 'Constitutional Guidelines for a Democratic South Africa', ANC policy paper, Lusaka, August 1988, doc. 153 in Gerhart and Glaser, *From Protest to Challenge, vol. 6*, 655. The proposed Bill of Rights guaranteed full political and civic rights to all citizens, imposed a duty on the state to eradicate economic and social inequalities produced as a result of discrimination, committed the country to a mixed economy, and specified rights for workers, women and families.

174 For discussion of the Guidelines, see Heidi Brooks, 'The African National Congress' Changing Relationship with Liberal Democracy' (MA thesis, Wits University, 2006), ch. 5.

175 Z.S.T. Skweyiya, 'Constitutional Guidelines of the ANC: A Vital Contribution to the Struggle against Apartheid', *Sechaba* 23, 6 (1989), 7.

176 A. Sachs (with intro by A. Astrow), 'Post-Apartheid South Africa: A Constitutional Framework', *World Policy Journal* 6, 3 (1989), 592, 593–4; Sachs, 'Towards a Bill of Rights for a Democratic South Africa', *Hastings International and Comparative Law Review* 12, 2 (1989), 293–4.

177 N. Haysom, 'Democracy, Constitutionalism, and the ANC's Bill of Rights for a New South Africa', *Social Justice* 18, 1–2 (1991), 41, 42.

178 www.anc.org.za.

179 Civil Rights League, *A South African Bill of Rights* (Cape Town, 1989), 17–21.

180 SAPA, 2.2.1993, report by Pierre Claassen.

181 Asmal, 'Democracy and Human Rights', 292; *Legacy of Freedom*.

182 A. Sachs, *Advancing Human Rights in South Africa* (Cape Town, 1992), 9, 17, 19.

Chapter 10: Setting the new nation to rights

183 In the case of the government, 'discovery' is more accurate than 'rediscovery'. For a representative discussion of the benefits and problems associated with a bill of rights, see the special issue of the *Columbia Human Rights Law Review* 21, 13 (1989–1990).

184 F. van Zyl Slabbert, 'Threats and Challenges to South Africa Becoming a More Open Society', in M. Shain (ed.), *Opposing Voices: Liberalism and Opposition in South Africa Today* (Johannesburg, 2006), 154–5; Klug, *Constituting Democracy*, 72.

185 Van der Vyver, who conferred with the ANC in Harare in 1989 as part of a lawyers' conference brokered by Idasa, informed me (pers. comm., 3.8.2010) that the ANC was 'dead against' a bill of rights at this time; though it did not take a great deal to convince the ANC representatives (who included Albie Sachs and Thabo Mbeki) that constitutional constraints on government power was 'a good thing'. By this time there were several key people in the ANC who were persuaded of the need for a Bill of Rights and the ANC had already published its Constitutional Guidelines. For an account of the Harare conference, see *Democracy in Action* (Idasa, February 1989).

186 Klug, *Constituting Democracy*, 48.

187 Atkinson, 'Insuring the Future?'

188 *Times Live*, 1.9.2011; 15.9.2011.

189 M. Chanock, *The Making of South African Legal Culture 1902–1936* (Cambridge, 2001), 533–4.

190 L. du Plessis, 'The South African Constitution as Memory and Promise', *Stellenbosch Law Review* 11 (2000), 385.

191 *Mail & Guardian*, 8.7.2011; See also Asmal, *Politics in My Blood*, 221–2.

192 The best explication of the TRC from a legal and anthropological perspective remains R. Wilson, *The Politics of Truth and Reconciliation in South Africa: Legitimizing the Post-Apartheid State* (Cambridge, 2001).

193 Wilson and Brown, 'Introduction', in *Humanitarianism and Suffering*, 21.

194 Wilson, *Politics of Truth and Reconciliation in South Africa*, 10, 13.

195 *Traces of Truth*, 'Reparations and Rehabilitation', www.truth.wwl.wits.ac.za.

196 Catherine Musuva, 'Democracy Protection Institutions in Southern Africa: South Africa's Public Protector and Human Rights Commission', EISA Research Report, no. 41 (Johannesburg, 2009).

197 L. Nathan, 'Interests, Ideas and Ideology: South Africa's Policy on Darfur', *African Affairs* 110, 438 (2011).

198 The achievements of the Constitutional Court are detailed in a magnificently produced book compiled by Lauren Segal and Sharon Cort, *One Law, One Nation* (Johannesburg, 2011).

199 *Mail & Guardian,* 10.11.2000, cited in S. Jensen, 'The South African Transition: From Development to Security?' *Development and Change* 36, 3 (2005), 563; 'Tshwete Challenges Human Rights Groups', *IOL News*, 4.11.1999, www.iol.co.za.

200 'You Said It, Mantashe', *Mail & Guardian*, 14.10.2008. See also Mantashe's accusation that the Constitutional Court is 'consolidating opposition to the government', *Cape Times*, 19.8.2011.

201 'In the Case of J Zuma and Others v the Constitution', *Business Day*, 30.9.2011; 'Constitution Reigns Whether Zuma Likes It or Not', *Business Day*, 31.8.2011.

202 'Talk delivered by Pierre de Vos on Tuesday 17 August 2010 at the Harold Wolpe Memorial Trust Event', www.constitutionallyspeaking.co.za.

203 Du Plessis, 'South African Constitution as Memory and Promise', 390.

204 I owe this point to the distinguished political philosopher and historian André du Toit. A Constitutional Court judgment in 2004 in a case brought by Lawyers for Human Rights determined that illegal immigrants were entitled to constitutional rights and protections.

205 J. Sarkin, 'The Development of a Human Rights Culture in South Africa', *Human Rights Quarterly* 20 (1998), 628.

206 Steven Robins, *From Revolution to Rights in South Africa* (Suffolk and Pietermaritzburg, 2008).

Index